CHRISTMAS 1989
TO UNK WITH LOVE, B———

AYCOCK BROWN'S OUTER BANKS

Aycock Brown's Outer Banks
Edited by David Stick

Design by Robert Cameron
Donning Company/Publishers, Inc.
Norfolk, Virginia Beach

**Library of Congress Cataloging-in-
Publication Data:**

Main entry under title:
Aycock Brown's Outer Banks.
1. Brown, Aycock. 2. Dare Co., N.C.—Biography. 3. Outer
Banks, N.C.—Biography. I. Brown, Aycock. II. Stick,
David, 1919-
F262.D2A9   975.6'275'0924   76-28296
ISBN 0-915442-18-3
ISBN 0-915442-17-5 de luxe
Printed in the United States of America

First Printing, November 1976
Second Printing, December 1976
Third Printing, April 1978
Fourth Printing, July 1986

CONTENTS

ACKNOWLEDGEMENTS

Aycock Brown estimates that he has taken more than one hundred thousand photographs of the Outer Banks. Finding a few hundred representative pictures for this book proved to be a more challenging task than any of us connected with the project had envisioned.

Sarah Owens, who has been Aycock's assistant for eighteen years, spent countless hours looking for pictures in the piles of old photo boxes Aycock ludicrously refers to as his filing system, and then somehow held him still long enough to put down information on names, dates, and locations.

Ina Evans was especially helpful in classifying pictures and determining which ones should go in specific chapters. Joyce Stone retyped all of the manuscript material, including the captions, and Mike Stick helped me edit all of the copy and double checked captions against the photographs which were to be used in the book. Rose and Penny Liverman assisted in a number of ways in the seemingly endless process of sorting out pictures and reassembling them in chapters.

The members of the Dare County Tourist Bureau special committee charged with responsibility for producing *Aycock Brown's Outer Banks* provided guidance and assistance as the book took shape. They are Marc Basnight, Ray Couch, Dan Elliot, and Bill Booker, in addition to Sarah Owens and Ina Evans.

Finally, special thanks to Aycock Brown for being Aycock Brown.

CONTRIBUTORS

David B. Eisendrath: photo consultant, *Time Magazine*
Lawrence Maddry: columnist, *Virginian-Pilot,* Norfolk, Virginia
Hugh Morton: president, *Grandfather Mountain,* Linville, North Carolina
Jim Mays: news editor, WTAR, Norfolk, Virginia
Roy Thompson: *Journal & Sentinel,* Winston-Salem, North Carolina
Joseph Baylor Roberts: retired photographer, *National Geographic*
John E. Blizzard: general manager, *Conquistador* outdoor drama, Arkansas
Gilbert Love: retired travel columnist, *Pittsburgh Press*
Bruce Roberts: author/photographer, Charlotte, North Carolina
Jack Aulis: columnist, *The News & Observer,* Raleigh, North Carolina
Woodrow Price: columnist and former managing editor, *The News & Observer,*
    Raleigh, North Carolina
John W. Fox: former general manager, *The Lost Colony* outdoor drama, Manteo,
    North Carolina
Richard Gonder: public editor, *The Virginian-Pilot,* Norfolk, Virginia
Francis Meekins: editor, *The Coastland Times,* Manteo, North Carolina
George Tames: photographer, *The New York Times*
Ollie Atkins: Washington editor, *The Saturday Evening Post*
Bill Wright: editor and publisher, *The State Magazine,* Raleigh, North Carolina
Hal Lyman: editor and publisher, *Salt Water Sportsman*
David Stick: North Carolina historian and author
Aycock Brown: photographer and publicist

INTRODUCTION

If you have never heard of Aycock Brown this book will tell you who he is and what he does.

If you have never had the good fortune to meet Aycock Brown this book will introduce you to him.

If you know Aycock, but have wondered along with the rest of us how he operates so effectively, this book will give you the answers.

First, for the record and for the uninitiated, Aycock Brown is the Manager and Publicity Director of the Dare County Tourist Bureau. No, that isn't exactly right, for there are those who claim in fact that Aycock Brown *is* the Dare County Tourist Bureau. Or, to put it another way, that the Dare County Tourist Bureau *is* Aycock Brown.

Maybe they're right, for the truth is that the Dare County Tourist Bureau was formed a quarter of a century ago for the sole and specific purpose of providing a vehicle with which Aycock Brown could get millions of dollars of free publicity for the Dare County Outer Banks on a budget which started out at ten thousand dollars a year. And he did it.

Good thing, too, for in 1950 before A.B. (before Aycock Brown, of course) North Carolina's long-isolated Outer Banks islands were facing a crisis. Commercial fishing and income from the United States Coast Guard service, long the joint backbones of the Outer Banks economy, were in decline, and a lot of people were betting their all that tourism would take up the slack.

Long-awaited modern roads and bridges were being built or planned to effectively link the Outer Banks with interior North Carolina and the rest of the world. The project to establish the nation's first national seashore recreational area—later to become the Cape Hatteras National Seashore—had been revived. And numerous new motels, hotels, restaurants, and other facilities were being constructed to accommodate the anticipated post-war tourist boom.

Unfortunately, there was more fizzle than oomph to the projected boom, and most of the facilities weren't doing enough business to meet expenses except at the peak of the short summer season.

Sensing a need to promote their new product, the operators of business facilities at the unincorporated coastal communities of Nags Head, Kill Devil Hills, and Kitty Hawk, and at the county seat of Manteo on Roanoke Island, had gone into the chamber of commerce business. Boy, had they gone into the chamber of commerce business. There was the Dare County Chamber of Commerce based in Manteo, the Dare Beaches Chamber of Commerce at Kitty Hawk, the new "Chamber of Commerce of Nags Head, Kill Devil Hills and Kitty Hawk, N. C., Inc." with offices in post office boxes in each community. All were actively competing for membership, business contributions, and tourist inquiries addressed to "Postmaster," but not accomplishing much else.

Since competing resorts from Virginia to Myrtle Beach were advertising extensively in newspapers and national magazines, one chamber group decided the Outer Banks obviously needed the same type of program. But when it was learned that a one page advertisement in a single issue of a leading magazine cost more than three times the total annual budget of the chamber, they figured there had to be a better way.

The better way they came up with was crudely simple. Instead of paying for expensive advertising they would get the same coverage in the same publications with free publicity. And they knew just the man to do the job.

Aycock Brown was a journeyman reporter-photographer, born in the mountains and reared in the piedmont, who had found his place—and an Ocracoke wife to share it with him—on the coast. After a succession of newspaper jobs he had turned to free-lancing for upstate papers and publicizing such Beaufort area establishments as Tony Seamon's now famous Sanitary Fish Market Restaurant.

Recently he had branched out, taking on clients ranging from *The Lost Colony* drama at Fort Raleigh on Roanoke Island, to a dog track at Moyock and a group promoting a toll road from Virginia Beach to Kitty Hawk, while still retaining clients in the Morehead City-Beaufort area. This schedule called for him to spend three days a week on the northern coast and three more days on the lower coast, and travel expenses seemed to eat up all the profit.

Thus, just at the time that hard-pressed tourist operators on the Dare coast were deciding they needed an Aycock Brown type to publicize their area, the original Aycock Brown had made up his mind that it was time to settle down.

The incorporation papers of the Dare County Tourist Bureau were filed in January 1952, with the objectives formally listed as required by law:

(a) To make known to tourists, vacationists, and sportsmen everywhere the multitude of natural and man-made attractions available in Dare County, and to induce them to visit the fascinating islands, the vast sounds, the attractive communities, the restored historical shrines, and the more than eighty miles of spectacularly beautiful coast line of Dare County.

(b) To secure the maximum publicity for Dare County through the establishment of a News Director office, and the employment of a qualified full-time News Director.

(c) To establish and maintain a central office for the dissemination of tourist information concerning all areas of Dare County and for the coordination of facilities serving those persons who visit Dare County.

As one of three incorporators of the Tourist Bureau, and its first secretary-treasurer, I shared responsibility in those days for raising the money to meet the Bureau's budget. There were some who felt the News Director's salary of a hundred dollars a week was exhorbitant, and that nobody could possibly spend the allocated thirty-two dollars per week on photographic expenses. Others, accustomed to fending for themselves in the highly competitive tourist business, and cognizant of the bitter feelings resulting from the battle between the various chambers of commerce, expressed scepticism that such a program could be conducted on a completely impartial and county-wide basis.

Twenty-five years later, tourism on the Dare Coast Outer Banks is the mainstay of the economy of the entire area, with millions of dollars spinning off annually to adjoining counties and Albemarle area cities.

Throughout this quarter of a century Aycock Brown's worth in publicizing the Outer Banks has been recognized by his peers in tourist promotion, who have repeatedly credited him with getting more publicity at less cost than anybody else in the business.

How he does it is something else again, and even those of us associated with Aycock and the Tourist Bureau from the outset have never really understood, for example, how he can take an ordinary picture of an ordinary looking girl holding an ordinary fish and get it published in hundreds of newspapers around the country.

This book, finally, tells how. Eighteen prominent editors, writers, and photographers who have been closely associated with Aycock through the years, provide unusual and searching insight into how he operates. Their frank appraisals have opened my eyes. They should open yours too.

David Stick, Kitty Hawk, North Carolina, Summer 1976

Aycock Brown at work in the late Sixties, complete with banana boat hat, perpetual squinting smile, pointing finger, and the ever-present cameras. (Photo by Emory Kristoff, courtesy National Geographic Society)

This action news picture of a Coast Guard helicopter lifting survivors from the trawler *Oriental* after it had foundered in the surf on south Bodie Island, won for Aycock two national prizes for news photography.

A TRIBUTE TO AYCOCK

by David B. Eisendrath
photo consultant, *Time Magazine*

From Ocracoke to Manteo,
    From inlet to the town,
The word is sped, the news is fed
    By hustling Aycock Brown.

Were triplets born in Hatteras?
    Did sailors wreck and drown?
The news is quickly gathered
    And sent on by Aycock Brown.

How big a marlin was weighed in?
    With polished verb and noun
The DISpatches are flashed world-wide
    By dashing Aycock Brown.

The actors of Lost Colony,
    Tragedian, mime or clown,
Appear in print from coast to coast:
    All thanks to Aycock Brown.

Who holds his camera very low
    When capturing smile or frown?
That belly-button portrait ace—
    Our Mathew Brady Brown.

Who juggles sixteen tasks at once
    And seldom can sit down—
Except to chit-chat with the friends
    Of charming Aycock Brown?

To pay a tribute to this scribe
    His friends of great renown
Are putting pen to paper here
    To honor Aycock Brown.

SALUTE, lean friend, OUR BEST TO YOU!
    With accolades we crown
Our Outer Banks' best publicist:
    WE LOVE YOU, AYCOCK BROWN.

THE COLORFUL CHARACTER NAMED BROWN

by Lawrence Maddry
columnist, *Virginian-Pilot,* Norfolk,
Virginia

If there is a more appropriate way for Dare County to celebrate our nation's bicentennial than by publishing a collection of Aycock Brown's photographs, then I'll jump backwards off Jockey's Ridge without a hang-glider.

That, incidentally, is the only way a newspaperman is going to get the jump on Aycock Brown.

For nearly thirty years this wizened Dare County Tourist Bureau director, who physically resembles Don Quixote, (in a Hawaiian sport shirt and banana boat hat, of course) has been jousting with newspapermen and outdoor writers the world over. And he wins every time.

Because of Brown, more has been written, photographed, and televised of that rugged stretch of dunes and sounds between Ocracoke and Duck, North Carolina, than any spot of similar size on earth.

Of course, that is his job. But there's nobody in the country that does it quite so well. He will get a story printed in your newspaper or magazine—*The New York Times,* or *The National Geographic,* it doesn't matter—by inundating you with his own stories or photographs, or completely knocking you off guard with the depth of his kindness, or spilling you into some deep well of laughter, pushed by the overwhelming force of his zany personality.

Those stories and films of the Cape Hatteras Lighthouse, *The Lost Colony,* the Wright Monument, and Ocracoke Harbor in a misty morning get printed because sooner or later nearly everybody in the news business finds himself in Aycock's debt. It is curious but it is so.

The last time I saw George Tames, the White House photographer for *The New York Times,* he was dangling one of Aycock's cameras from his neck. "He beats anything I ever saw," Tames said.

When I worked in Raleigh there were days when Aycock's photographs were competing with really good shots from around the state for newspaper space.

An editor would look at one with Aycock Brown's name on it and tell the desk man to run it. "It's not that good," he'd say, "but Aycock's going to raise hell if I don't print it or else fill my mailbox with shipments of those Dare County figs. I don't know which is worse."

I believe the first time I met Aycock was in the side yard of his home in Manteo. I had been employed as a reporter for *The Coastland Times,* and, after introducing himself, Aycock continued with one of his usual bizarre projects.

He was setting out some of the ugliest artwork that ever came from a brick kiln. Naturally they had to do with the Outer Banks. They were gold statues of Virginia Dare. They were horrible kewpie-doll-like figures resembling Raquel Welch.

"Jeez, did you ever see anything so beautiful," Aycock said. "Fellow up the street here was selling 'em. I bought all he had, two dozen."

A man of boundless energy, he was suddenly darting about the yard—a human dragonfly, dropping those statues like eggs under every tree, bush, and shrub in the yard. As he disappeared in a privet hedge, he turned and, with characteristic generosity, shouted: "Don't go away. I want to give you one!"

A few days later I stepped into his office, a small room in the Dare County Community Building which he has occupied for about twenty years, that never changes. Like Brown, the room literally spills over with information about Dare County. The walls are a-clutter with photographs of the Wright Brothers or chesty bathing beauties in languorous poses beside the Atlantic.

As I entered, Brown was reaching into his pocket and handing over a ten dollar bill to a perfect stranger. The man was a vacationer on the Outer Banks who claimed that he needed the money to make bus fare to his home in New Jersey. Brown has been doing this kind of thing for years, claiming that people always pay him back. I doubt it.

"I never did anything for anybody that didn't reap to my benefit about tenfold; it has something to do with casting your bread upon the waters like it says in the Bible," he said. "It's funny, but it really works."

This said, he returned to the clutter of his desk, probing beneath the press releases he'd been writing since six a.m. for a package of cigarettes.

"Mr. Brown," I said, "I want you to tell me about your life, it might make a good story for *The Coastland Times*."

A smile creased the tiny corner of his mouth the cigarette didn't occupy.

"Hell, Maddry," he said, "You'll never make anything out of my life. It's a perfect muddle." Which, of course, it is.

Running true to form, Brown was born in the mountains of North Carolina, near Blowing Rock. The family later moved to Hillsborough, where his father was manager of Occoneechee Farm. After high school he found a job as reporter on the *Elizabeth City Independent,* a wildcat publication ideally suited for a man of Brown's temperament. Soon after his arrival in Elizabeth City, Brown began courting the editor's daughter and left, he said, just in time to avoid being fired.

He wandered to New York, then settled down in Greenwich Village, where he took journalism courses at Columbia University. Earning money for school with part-time jobs, he not only shoveled snow and sold insurance, but once unloaded a boatload of goat hides from Persia. "Nobody would sit next to me the next day in class. I couldn't understand it," he recalled.

After two years in the North, he returned to North Carolina and paid a call on O. H. (Skipper) Coffin, who then was editor of *The Raleigh Times*.

"Coffin took me up to the Capitol. I remember how he walked into the governor's office unannounced, put his foot up on the desk, said something like 'Hi Mac' to Governor Angus McLean. It beat anything I'd ever heard of, and I decided right then I was going to be a newsman no matter what."

After an unsuccessful stint as police reporter for the *Durham Herald,* Brown moved to the coast and has been there since. In 1928 he acquired the kind of job he does best—promoting Atlantic Beach, North Carolina. But he grew tired of the job and set out for Ocracoke, where he was offered two weeks free lodging for writing publicity pieces about the place. He stayed there seven years.

He was charmed by the colorful characters who swapped yarns on the docks at Ocracoke Harbor, the slap of the Atlantic on the lonely beaches, and the haunted isolation of the sleepy village in winter. He also learned that it was island custom to make your own coffin, and later wrote a major story about it that appeared in *The Saturday Evening Post*.

Ocracoke was also the place where he met Esther Styron, the girl he was later to marry. "I was running bootleg booze from Morehead City, and when we pulled into Ocracoke Harbor in a skiff she was standing on the dock. I don't think I ever saw anybody as pretty in my whole life," he said. "I'll tell you how pretty she was. For several minutes I completely forgot about all those gallons of liquor in the boat. And it was good stuff."

With his knowledge of Ocracoke, Brown also started an island newspaper (he published in Beaufort) and augmented his income by selling tourists seashells which he had improved with India ink. "You know they were bad, but a tourist will buy anything," he confides.

He also started a column called "Covering the Waterfront," which was carried by a number of North Carolina papers. Soon afterward he left to become editor of the Beaufort, North Carolina paper, where he startled visitors by keeping a pet crocodile on his desk.

Before leaving Ocracoke, Brown had all his upper teeth pulled by an itinerant dentist who performed his services free. Unable to afford an upper plate, he grew the slim, bristling mustache which has become his trademark, so his mouth wouldn't look funny. Today he wears an upper plate, but friends say his mouth still looks irregular. That is because he is always talking.

This garrulous trait served him well in Beaufort, where he earned money for his family by reading the news to moviegoers at a local theater during the days of Bank Nights at the movies.

"They'd play a spotlight onto the stage and I'd stay out of sight reading into a microphone. I was billed as 'Aycock Brown—the Voice From the Silver Screen," he recalls.

During World War II Brown was a civilian intelligence officer with the Navy, specializing in the removal of dead bodies from the oil soaked beaches and spotting for U-boat activity. "There were hundreds of people arriving in lifeboats at Ocracoke burned and scarred when their ships were torpedoed. I don't think I'll ever forget the horror in their eyes," he remembers.

After the war, Brown returned to the publicity business, writing his daily column and scouting the North Carolina coastland for stories. It was Brown who first wrote of the wild pony roundups on Ocracoke, for instance, and the restaurant that has almost become a Tar Heel institution—the Sanitary Fish Market in Morehead City.

In 1948, he was hired to publicize *The Lost Colony* in Manteo. He has been in Dare County ever since.

The Dare County Brown is so multifaceted that it is impossible to capture all his activities. There is Brown the excellent photographer, who once became so preoccupied while taking a picture of dignitaries visiting the Elizabethan Gardens that he fell from a tree and broke his arm.

There is Aycock Brown the Banker's friend, sending Christmas presents to widows every Christmas, introducing newspapermen to every character he passes on the street as a possible news story. "Well, if you don't want to write about old Jed here, write about his granddaddy. Jed, tell this newsman about the dream your daddy had two nights before the wreck of the *Mirlo* at Hatteras."

There is the Aycock Brown who serves as lay reader at St. Andrews By-the-Sea and the Brown who pauses beside a windswept dune near Hatteras for several minutes, rather than drive by a place so incredibly beautiful with the reddish tinge of sunset, bristling marsh grass, all wrapped in a gauze of evening fog.

But above all there is Aycock Brown the character, the coastal promotions expert who neither swims nor fishes.

"Oh, I like looking at the ocean all right," he once told me. "It's just that I don't care to swim in it. Of course millions do. The truth is, it's always looked filthy to me."

If Maddry ever tries to jump backwards off Jockey's Ridge—with or without a hang glider—the one known factor is that Aycock would be there to snap a picture of the event, as he did these hang gliders taking off (upper right), in flight (center) and getting ready to climb Jockey's Ridge for another jump (bottom).

Aycock has taken pictures of Cape Hatteras Lighthouse from every conceivable angle—and had dozens of them published all over the world. This one taken from a small plane is one of his favorites, showing the spiraled sentinel in the foreground with the menacing Graveyard of the Atlantic beyond.

The first step in photographic promotion is taking the picture, the second is having it published, and the third is getting your sales message across in the accompanying caption. Aycock is a master at all three, as this 1971 caption shows:

SCENE FROM THE LOST COLONY—The colonists board ship at Plymouth, England to begin their voyage to the New World in this performance photograph from *The Lost Colony*. The outdoor drama is presented each summer in Waterside Theatre on Roanoke Island where the first English settlements in America were located. Performance dates for 1971 are June 23 through August 28. (Photo by Aycock Brown)

The nation's editors seem as obsessed with printing pictures of the Wright Brothers Monument National Memorial as Aycock is with taking them; and year after year he comes up with new perspectives, new angles and new backgrounds to meet the demand.

With old Ocracoke lighthouse in the background and the sun glistening on the wavelets of Silver Lake in the foreground, Aycock catches a shot of the Cedar Island ferry entering the harbor with its cargo of automobiles and sightseers.

Aycock was one of the originators of the Dare County Tourist Bureau's Dare Coast Pirate Jamboree, an annual spring event which provided him with unusual photographic subject matter over a span of more than a decade. An early "pirate" king, John Donoho, is pictured here on the left with one of his crewmen, the late Dr. Wallace Mustian.

A widely used Aycock Brown photograph combines his favorite picture ingredients—pretty girls, the gentle Outer Banks surf, and a gimmick. In this early 1950s picture the gimmick is starfish which the smiling girls apparently are considering for earrings.

Outer Banks fish and cute children are favorite lens subjects, and when the two can be combined effectively there is no question the picture will be published.

Aycock can take pretty pictures, especially with pretty girls to make them even prettier. This tranquil scene is at Manns Harbor on the Dare County mainland.

During Aycock's reign on the Outer Banks there have
been only a handful of remaining "banker ponies," but
a year has never passed without his getting "banker
pony" pictures printed in the nation's newspapers. This
was an early one in the 1940s at one of the last "pony
pennings," on Cape Lookout.

American newspaper readers seem fascinated with
accounts of modern day shipwrecks, so editors never
fail to run shipwreck pictures, frequently as not on the
front page. And few ships have encountered trouble off
the Outer Banks in the past three decades without
Aycock's camera being called into play.

People associated with Aycock over the years have often wondered if he ever relaxes. Yes he does, and at such times he indulges in his favorite avocation: taking pictures of flowers and birds.

One of Aycock's first successful public relations ventures was promoting Tony Seaman's Sanitary Fish Market Restaurant at Morehead City. Aycock took this picture of Tony in the restaurant, which has become one of the largest and best known seafood restaurants on the cast coast.

Aycock gives editors wide latitude in running pictures. For example, they could print this one any way they wanted—upside down, sideways, or right side up; just so long as they printed it. And by turning the page the reader can decide which way he likes it best.

"I stepped into his office," Lawrence Maddry writes in the accompanying sketch, "a small room in the Dare County Community Building which he has occupied for about twenty years, that never changes. Like Brown, the room literally spills over with information about Dare County. The walls are a-clutter with photographs of the Wright Brothers or chesty bathing beauties in languorous poses beside the Atlantic." Aycock is subject for a change, rather than photographer, in this early 1970s photo. (Photo by Jim Bramlett)

The idea for the Elizabethan Garden adjacent to Fort Raleigh on Roanoke Island did not originate with Aycock, but if the women of The Garden Club of North Carolina, Inc. had not come up with the idea, Aycock probably would have, for the gardens have provided him with innumerable photo subjects, every month of the year. The Lost Colony's Queen Elizabeth greets a properly costumed subject, while Aycock takes advantage of an improperly costumed statue of Virginia Dare. The sculptured fish net is fairly authentic.

Next to flying and taking pictures, few things hold as much fascination for Aycock as bridges, lighthouses, and the ever changing waters adjacent to his beloved Outer Banks. He must have derived special pleasure from this aerial photograph of the Oregon Inlet bridge and surrounding waters, with Bodie Island Lighthouse miniscule in the background.

"It's not that good," the editor would say, "but Aycock's going to raise hell if I don't print it or else fill my mailbox with a shipment of those Dare County figs. I don't know which is worse." So, as Lawrence Maddry explains, newspaper readers end up seeing another Aycock Brown picture, this one of surf fishermen and beach buggies on a blustery Outer Banks fall morning.

Sand dunes, sea oats, and surf, a sure fire combination to capture an editor's fancy.

HE TAKES THE MAIL
TO THE POST OFFICE

by Hugh Morton
president, *Grandfather Mountain,*
Linville, North Carolina

The late Bill Sharpe was probably the closest friend I had whom I shared with Aycock Brown. Both Aycock and I idolized Bill for his great writing and story-telling ability, and for the tremendous contribution he made in the formative years of the North Carolina travel promotion program. Bill Sharpe thought the world of Aycock.

We were at one of the Honorary Tar Heel meetings at the Carolinian Hotel, where several of Aycock's writer and photographer friends were gathered in a bull and drinking session, with Aycock not in the room at the moment. The photographers present, I believe, were Johnny Hemmer, Alfred DeLardi, Bob Garland, Larry Williams, Joe Costa, Ollie Atkins, and George Tames, as well as myself. Someone in the group asked Bill Sharpe how it was possible for Aycock to get so many of his stories and pictures published. Bill's explanation was in my view very perceptive, and I confess it has had a pronounced affect on my life for the past twenty-five years, in my own efforts to publicize various projects.

Bill said what we all knew, that Aycock had turned up many exceptional stories and numerous great pictures, but that sometimes they were not particularly outstanding, and they were run anyway. Bill said that the stories and pictures were there on the desk when the newspapers and magazines wanted them, and that each editor had been made to feel by Aycock that Aycock was serving as his extra staff member on the Outer Banks, looking after the editor's interests. The editors were reluctant not to run Aycock's stuff, Bill said, because they could not risk disrupting the momentum of the incessant flow of words and pictures that would otherwise not be coming from any other source on the coast.

Then Bill Sharpe penetrated the heart of the Aycock Brown success. He said: "If there is one thing above all which has contributed to Aycock's effectiveness as a publicity man for the Outer Banks, it is the fact that he takes the mail to the post office."

Those words by Bill Sharpe were the gospel as far as I am concerned, and applicable to Aycock Brown and all other persons who aspire to do a good job in the publicity field. The methods of publicizing have changed some in the twenty-five years that have transpired. Television back then was really not a factor, but Aycock's "secret" of taking the mail to the post office hasn't been improved upon. Well, on second thought, strike that statement. Aycock, like the rest of us, had found by 1976 that United Parcel Service was often a more reliable courier of publicity materials than the United States Mail. Repetitive, consistent volume was what Bill Sharpe was talking about, however, and at that Aycock was master.

No person will ever know how much in actual dollar value Aycock Brown has added to the tax books of Dare and some of North Carolina's other coastal counties, but it is up in the millions. Some may want to debate whether this is good or bad, but I say it was good at the time he did it. The area was one of the very lowest on the per capita income scale when Aycock began his great work. The area is still lower than it ought to be, but it is infinitely better than it was before Aycock first came on the scene.

When I see a public figure like Richard M. Nixon really blow it, I often think how the course of history could have been changed if he had had on his staff Aycock Brown, and had listened to him. Aycock knows that the only lie you tell the press is the first one, and that after that, you are dead. He also lives by another rule that I have steadfastly tried to follow: "Do not ever become involved in a fight with a newspaper unless you own a bigger newspaper." (This applies to radio stations and television stations as well.) My, how Mr. Nixon and the others could have benefited. Aycock Brown could have served them well.

Throughout his photographic career Aycock has roamed the Outer Banks, in jeeps, cars, boats, planes, and on foot—camera always ready to catch interesting subjects, especially boats and fishermen. This one shows the trawler fleet at Wanchese on Roanoke Island, at rest on a winter weekend.

The mail and passenger boat *Aleta,* which operated daily for many years between Ocracoke and Portsmouth on the Outer Banks and the mainland community of Atlantic. This picture was taken in the mid 1940s.

Aycock caught these two trawlers, the *Esther Joy* and the *Mitzi Kay,* anchored at Oregon Inlet, waiting for favorable tide conditions to move to offshore fishing waters through the shoally inlet.

Home from the sea, their holds filled with fish, the ships of the trawler fleet head back toward Oregon Inlet, led by the *Wayne Laurin.*

For more than a quarter of a century Outer Banks fishermen, local officials, and businessmen have been fighting for approval of the so-called Oregon Inlet Project. Designed to provide a stable all-weather channel through the inlet and modern port facilities at nearby Wanchese, the project is now nearing reality. In this scene the trawler *Irma Virginia* of Gloucester Point, Virginia, and the *Faith Evelyn* of Wanchese are tied up side by side, showing how crowded the little port can be during the offshore fishing season.

Three seagulls, each on his own private perch, stand sentinel over the charter boat fleet at the Oregon Inlet Fishing Center. The Center, owned by the National Park Service, but leased to private operators, is headquarters for what has been described as a million dollar fleet of Gulf Stream charter boats.

Part of the charter fleet at anchor in the Oregon Inlet Fishing Center, showing the old ferry dock, lower right, and the Oregon Inlet Bridge in the background.

One of the pioneers in establishing charter boat service for Gulf Stream fishing from Outer Banks ports was Ernal Foster of Hatteras, owner of the *Albatross* charter boat fleet. This picture, made by a photographer for the State Advertising Division in color as a cover for a fishing booklet, shows Foster, left, and Aycock Brown as models. Though he says he has taken "tens of thousands" of fishing pictures, Aycock swears he has only gone fishing twice, and both times reluctantly. The first trip, to the Gulf Stream, was with Captain Joe Berry, and the second with his son Captain Billy Brown. (Photo courtesy North Carolina Travel and Promotion Division)

Initially sports fishermen interested in chartering boats for Gulf Stream fishing had to make arrangements with the owners of small commercial fishing boats. Beginning in the late 1930s a few of these boats were fitted out for sports fishing in the summer and commercial fishing in the winter, a practice almost unheard of today when dozens of specially designed boats make up the charter fleet. This picture shows the late Captain Fred Basnight's *Slow An Easy* gliding into tranquil Wanchese Harbor in the 1950s with a catch of crabs. During the sports fishing season the *Slow An Easy* was converted into a charter boat.

Boatbuilding on the Outer Banks is both an art and a craft, the skills and pride of workmanship passed down from father to son, generation after generation. At Phillips Boat Yard and Marine Supply Company in Wanchese, Aycock took this 1975 picture of the launching of the cruiser *Follow The Sun*, built by Allen Hayman and Bobby Sullivan.

Fishermen interested in trying their luck in the Gulf Stream, which passes within fourteen miles of Cape Hatteras, can charter a modern sports fishing boat, complete with a captain to tell them how to fish and a mate to put on the bait and take off the catch; or they can book passage for a fraction of the cost on a headboat like the *Big G,* shown backing into Oden's Docks at Hatteras in this 1969 picture.

The innumerable sounds, bays, and creeks which make up the vast estuarine system adjacent to the Outer Banks attract fishermen of all ages. In the Kitty Hawk Bay area, a boy poles his skiff over the still surface, while his little passenger keeps a watchful eye on the photographer.

Everybody seems to fish on the Outer Banks, and seemingly almost anyplace they can get to the water. While boats of the charter fleet return to port a fisherman with one line already overboard goes about the business of baiting a back-up, just in case.

One of the oldest and best known vessels on the Banks, the *Hattie Creef* made regular freight runs between Roanoke Island and Elizabeth City, with side trips to other fishing communities, soon after the turn of the century. Beached at last, the *Hattie Creef* is shown here being moved to a new location as a tourist attraction by John Ferebee, Manteo businessman and house mover. The old vessel, which is reputed to have hauled supplies for the Wright Brothers, is now part of a restaurant complex at Salvo, North Carolina.

Since the earliest days of settlement the sea has been a source of income for residents of the Outer Banks, yielding its harvest of fish to those willing and able to launch their small wooden dories through the surf to set their nets beyond. In an early and popular photograph Aycock framed the beached dory in the left foreground with the fishermen silhouetted beyond as they hauled their net above the wash and loaded their catch on a truck rigged up as a beach buggy.

Spot and mullet are loaded into the back of the truck in preparation for the trip to the fish house, and payday.

Sailboats, long the basic mode of transportation among
Outer Banks communities, have gained new popularity
for those seeking recreational solitude.

Annual sailing regattas in Croatan Sound attract par-
ticipants from several states. This one in 1970 also
attracted a number of fly-in sailors at the Manteo Airport, with Aycock looking on from aloft.

UNADULTERATED, PASSIONATE, ETERNAL LOVE

by Jim Mays
news editor, WTAR, Norfolk, Virginia

Any man who can make the main street of Manteo, North Carolina, sound like a breathlessly exciting place has a special kind of talent. Aycock Brown knows how to do that.

It's not that Manteo isn't exciting, of course. It's just that Aycock knows how to create more excitement than meets the eye in Manteo.

He also knows how to conjure up via long-distance telephone a compelling conviction in the minds of faraway journalists that a dead whale washed up on the beach at Rodanthe is a story of major international significance.

I have been a student of Aycock's for nearly thirty years now, and I still haven't figured out how he does it. One thing I do know. He is the only man I have ever known who can do it.

Maybe you can get some idea of his skill as a publicist by recalling with me the blistering summer afternoon when the famous *Life* magazine photographer David Douglas Duncan and I stood for four hours on the Currituck Sound Bridge waiting for a porpoise to roll so that we could take a picture of it. Finally, about four o'clock, I said to Duncan: "Can you tell me why we are standing here baking our brains out waiting for a porpoise?"

"Sure," said Duncan. "Aycock said to."

Then there was the time early in his career when Aycock decided that a hurricane in the West Indies was going to hit the Outer Banks. With the hurricane thousands of miles away, Aycock had some thirty or so reporters and photographers sitting on top of Jockey Ridge on a cloudless afternoon, peering through binoculars at the horizon where Aycock assured everyone present the hurricane probably would show up at any moment.

It never did show up! But Aycock, as always, was equal to the occasion. He saw to it that the journalists went back to their home offices loaded with pictures and stories lauding the lure and lore and legends of the Outer Banks. Among the knowing, Aycock's performance on that occasion is still referred to as Brown's Hurricane.

How does he do it? I haven't the foggiest notion, really. But after three decades as an Aycock Brown observer, I do have some estimates.

First, is his outrageously infectious enthusiasm for the Outer Banks. He has an absolutely remarkable capacity for convincing you that the most important thing in life is getting a good picture of a piece of broken shell with the Cape Hatteras Lighthouse in the background.

His enthusiasm for the Outer Banks, I think, springs from devotion. No, not devotion. Love. Pure unadulterated, passionate, eternal love. Love for every grain of sand, every wash of surf, every tumble of foam and spindrift, every cut, channel, sandbar, and sprig of dune grass, every toll of Bell Buoy and flash from the Currituck Bridge to Portsmouth Island.

Few men, I think, have been fortunate enough to have a love affair like this with a place. Even fewer, having found such a place, would deliberately devote their lives to sharing it with the rest of the world. But come to think of it, that's the most unselfish love of all, isn't it?

Along with his love for his chosen part of the country goes his irrepressible, inexhaustible energy. I never have been able to find out when—or if—he ever sleeps. But I firmly believe that if a surf angler fishing alone at midnight in that deep slough just north of Avon were to catch a sixty-pound channel bass, Aycock would shortly pop over the dune and start posing the proud angler with his hefty catch for flash pictures which would make the afternoon editions in Toledo, Buffalo, Memphis, and maybe even San Francisco.

If the editors of this book hadn't specifically instructed me not to write a tribute to Aycock, I would mention his eternal cheerfulness and optimism, his humility, his considerateness, his kindness, his generosity, and a dozen other qualities most of the rest of us could benefit from emulating.

They said not to write a tribute. They said just to tell about experiences with Aycock. It can't be done. If you admire Aycock as I do, when you relate an experience with him, it always winds up a tribute.

"He also knows," says Jim Mays, "how to conjure up via long-distance telephone a compelling conviction in the minds of faraway journalists that a dead whale washed up on the beach at Rodanthe is a story of major international significance." Typically, this one wasn't the greatest whale photograph ever made, but the editors ran it anyway.

Some of Aycock's earliest Outer Banks photographs were of Ocracoke Lighthouse, one of the oldest lighthouses in America still in active use. One of his pictures of Ocracoke light was a decoration on the wall of the American Embassy in Mexico City, when Josephus Daniels was Ambassador.

Teach's Hole at Ocracoke reputedly was the hideout of the pirate Blackbeard, who was killed and beheaded in a battle just beyond. Aycock frames the Ocracoke lighthouse in the background for this eerie effect.

Tourists and Cape Hatteras Islanders join together at the base of the lighthouse for festivities.

When Stuart Udall, then Secretary of Interior, visited Cape Hatteras in 1963, Aycock posed him in front of the massive structure with a miniature reproduction in hand. So mariners can distinguish them, each lighthouse has different markings or colors ranging from the spiralling black and white stripes at Cape Hatteras, to the horizontal stripes at Bodie Island, the diamonds at Cape Lookout, and the solid red brick at Currituck.

Famous Cape Hatteras Lighthouse, described as "the most imposing and substantial brick lighthouse on this continent, if not in the world," when constructed in 1870, is a favorite photographic subject. During his years on the coast Aycock has employed every conceivable gimmick and angle in taking pictures of the lighthouse for publication. In this early one, he poses a Hatteras Island belle on the foundation of the old Cape Hatteras Lighthouse, which was destroyed during the Civil War.

Even when disaster strikes the Outer Banks, Aycock takes advantage of the situation to come up with pictures he feels the nation's editors will publish. In this instance he showed the effects of erosion on manmade protective sand dunes near The Point at Cape Hatteras, with the ever-present lighthouse in the background.

This picture of the Corolla Post Office with Currituck Beach Lighthouse in the background was taken in the early 1950s. The man shown standing is John Austin, at that time the Postmaster and storekeeper, and at this time still a resident of the isolated community on the Currituck banks.

Bodie Island Lighthouse, just north of Oregon Inlet, was constructed in 1872, the third federal lighthouse structure in that area. The building which formerly housed the lighthouse keeper and his family is now a natural history museum operated by the National Park Service. Each of the major lighthouses on the coast was designed to be easily identified by mariners at night by controlling the frequency of successive flashes of the beacon.

In addition to the tall lighthouses on shore, supposedly spaced at intervals along the coast so that the mariner would pick up the one ahead before he lost sight of the one behind him, there have been efforts for more than 150 years to provide a warning light on the outer fringes of Diamond Shoals at Cape Hatteras. Plans were made in 1890 to replace the lightship with a tower rising 150 feet above the shoals, but were abandoned. Finally, in the 1960s, a Texas tower type platform was erected, and the Diamond Shoals lightship was retired from service.

Providing free library service to all residents of Dare County was accomplished with the purchase of the world's first—and probably the world's only—four-wheel drive bookmobile, shown here on its maiden run, with the Cape Hatteras Lighthouse as backdrop. Helen Meekins Midgett of Roanoke Island was the librarian-driver.

When ferry service was established across Oregon Inlet in the 1920s mail, freight and passengers were still carried to and from Manteo by boat. Then the Midgett brothers of Hatteras started their bus line, with daily runs up the beach from Hatteras Village to Manteo, and more rapid and reliable transportation was at last available for passengers. This picture shows an early Midgett bus loading passengers in front of the old Hatteras Post Office.

43

As the years passed the Midgett brothers, Anderson, Stockton, and Harold, incorporated their business, changed the name from "Manteo-Hatteras" to "Hatteras-Manteo" and began using larger buses. They still had to pick the best route available in areas where there were no roads, either following sandy tracks in the interior route, or driving close to the beach, as in this picture in which Aycock added three of his favorite ingredients—pretty girls, an old shipwreck, and the Outer Banks surf in the background. The girls were Sally Alford, Lydia Love, and Sarah Alford (now Mrs. Sarah Owens and Aycock's longtime "girl Friday").

Since early colonial days it has been a responsibility of government to supervise the disposition of the cargo of wrecked vessels. This auction-type sale was called a vendue, presided over by a vendue master or Wreck Commissioner. The late Alpheus W. Drinkwater, long-time telegrapher at Manteo, served for many years as Wreck Commissioner, and presided over this sale. He is shown here at left, in the overcoat.

The nameplate was one of the most prized items to be salvaged from Outer Banks shipwrecks, and the Fearing family of Elizabeth City decorated their Nags Head Soundside cottage with nameplates from vessels wrecked on the Outer Banks.

When at last paved roads were constructed to most communities in the Outer Banks area a big boom in real estate development soon followed. Aycock took this picture at the north end community on Colington Island, showing residences and the community graveyard, shortly after the sandy trail was paved, but before the large Colington Harbour development was begun.

This aerial photograph of Cape Point shows the Cape Hatteras Lighthouse, and the narrow area just beyond, known in early days as "The Haulover," and site of the temporary inlet which opened during the Ash Wednesday Storm in 1962. At the time the picture was taken the National Park Service was experimenting with protective measures at Cape Point. Part of the village of Buxton is visible at upper left, with naval facility and early resort development just beyond the lighthouse, and the Loran station in the center.

AN UNPUBLISHED GUIDEBOOK TO HIS PART OF THE NORTH CAROLINA COAST

by Roy Thompson
Journal & Sentinel, Winston-Salem,
North Carolina

Aycock Brown has the look of a somewhat scholarly pirate whose ship has sailed and left him high and dry.

At first casual glance he appears to be the luckless sort of chap that muscle men kick sand on at the beach.

But not so....

This Boone of the dunes is a giant of a man—a trailblazer who has led the outside world to the Lost Colony and the previously little-known wonders of the Dare Coast of North Carolina.

Aycock Brown has made Dareland known among the inhabitants of every city and crossroads from Miami to Montreal and west to the nigh bank of the Mississippi.

How?

David Stick asked the question in seeking a few words about Aycock to be printed along with his pictures:

"How can he take an ordinary picture of an ordinary girl holding an ordinary fish and get it printed in hundreds of newspapers?"

It should be understood at once that Aycock Brown has hundreds of friends who would try to get his pictures into their newspapers if the pictures showed old beer bottles on a garbage pile.

Now let it be said in addition that while the fish Aycock takes pictures of may be ordinary enough, there is nothing ordinary about the girls holding those ordinary fish. Aycock's models fairly erupt with lavish extraordinariness of the special kind most cherished by picture editors, most of whom are male chauvinists who get to the beach seldom and then have to take their wives.

Aycock poses his bathing-suited girls in front of gnarled oaks...in front of beached ships...alongside defeated marlin...and in front of the newly-elected officers of one benevolent and/or fraternal organization after another.

If Aycock were assigned to photograph the gala opening of the new men's room at the YMCA he would have one of his models standing in the door, and you could bet she'd be one of the previously undiscovered natural wonders of this well-traveled world.

Another thing about this man....He is an unpublished guidebook to his part of the North Carolina coast. He knows the answers to ten thousand and one most-often-asked questions about Dareland, and if someone asks a question that Aycock cannot answer, he answers it anyway.

This is to keep his record perfect.

Aycock knows the place to stay, the place to eat, the way to charter a boat to go drink beer on and maybe fish for marlin, the place to get a broken reel mended...an unruly head of hair beautified...a quickie marriage arranged.

He was an authority on the habitat of local bootleggers until the State of North Carolina and the County of Dare socialized the local liquor business, driving any number of free enterprisers into other lines of work.

Any number of writers, photographers, itinerant politicians, and other far-wanderers drop in on Aycock every week. They are drawn to him the way small children are drawn to mud puddles and gift counters.

Aycock can always help.

Aycock always does.

He has combed the beaches, dunes, and sounds of Dare in tireless search of camera subjects that—with the thoughtful placing of one of his super girls in the foreground—might snag some picture space that might otherwise have been given to Henry Kissinger's leaving an airplane here or there.

He has probably met more boats than United States customs agents have.

He knows where the Mother Vineyard is...how far it is to the nearest cold beer from any given geographical position in northeast North Carolina...what the governor of North Carolina said to the governor of South Carolina...when the snow geese are expected on Hatteras...and I don't know what all.

Dare County and I have a great deal in common.

We both owe Aycock Brown a lot.

Roy Thompson explains that Aycock Brown has hundreds of editor friends who would run in their papers almost anything Aycock sent. This picture, described by Aycock as one of the first historic markers erected by the State Historical Commission, was run by a number of his editor friends. The marker originally stood near the entrance to Fort Raleigh before major changes were made in providing access to the national historic site a few years back.

Old tombstones aren't exactly front page news, but since this one in the Howard Graveyard at Ocracoke states that Warren O. Wahab died thirteen years before he was born, it was widely published. The inscription states: "Born September 10th 1855. Died September 11th 1842."

Aycock admits he is a sucker for an Outer Banks sunset. This one, over Pond Island on the Roanoke Sound Bridge causeway, is one of many he has taken through the years.

Special ceremonies are held at Kill Devil Hills each year on December 17, the anniversary of the Wright Brothers' first successful flights in a heavier than air machine, December 17, 1903. Aycock begins his annual promotion of the event in late summer, building up to the grand—and almost always cold—finale in December. This picture, circa 1950, shows three military planes flying over the Wright Brothers National Memorial and those gathered on top of Kill Devil Hill for the event.

The Roanoke Colony Memorial Association erected this tablet at Fort Raleigh in 1896, marking the supposed site of the Raleigh colonists' fort, as well as the birth of Virginia Dare, first child born of English parents in America, and her baptism. Confirmation that this was, in fact, the site of the fort, resulted from extensive archeological excavations under the direction of Dr. J. C. Harrington of the National Park Service. A reproduction of the colonists' fort is behind the marker.

In this 1952 picture Aycock caught a stormy sea pounding at the wreckage of the schooner *Laura S. Barnes.* The vessel foundered on Bodie Island in 1921, and became a popular tourist attraction after establish-

ment of the Cape Hatteras National Seashore. Fearful that the sea would once again claim the remnant of the vessel, the National Park Service has moved the wreckage to higher ground at Coquina Beach near Oregon Inlet.

The maiden voyage of the *Seven Eleven* in 1975 apparently ended in tragedy when she drifted ashore below Oregon Inlet after being abandoned at sea by her crew. Aycock says "she seemed to be unsalvageable" when he took this picture, but she was subsequently gotten off the beach by Basnight Construction Company of Manteo, using heavy equipment to dig out around her at low tide.

Annual coverage of Paul Green's outdoor drama *The Lost Colony,* at Waterside Theatre, near the site of the first attempt at English colonization on the north end of Roanoke Island, generally begins soon after the last performance of the season, building up to the opening performance in June the next year. This is a widely used picture showing some of the many actors in the costumes they wear in the drama.

An eleventh century fountain forms a centerpiece for what Aycock describes as a "Knot Garden" in the Elizabethan Garden near Fort Raleigh. "Knot Gardens" are said to have been common on the larger estates during the Elizabethan era of English history.

Pea Island National Wildlife Refuge, on the north end of Hatteras Island, is the winter resting place for thousands of Greater Snow Geese. When Aycock learned that some had gone beyond their normal southern range he located them in a tidal pond just back of Cape Point at Hatteras, and maneuvered as usual to catch the famed lighthouse as a backdrop.

Toll-free state-owned ferries maintain regular schedules across Hatteras Inlet, connecting Ocracoke Island with Hatteras. Gulls follow the ferry boats back and forth across the inlet, looking for handouts from passengers. Some have become tame enough to be hand fed, as in this picture, and most have become proficient at catching thrown morsels of bread or crackers in flight.

Lifeboat stations of the United States Lifesaving Service were erected along the Outer Banks at seven mile intervals beginning in the 1880s. The United States Coast Guard was formed with the merger of the Lifesaving Service and the Revenue Service in 1914, and all of the old stations were replaced by larger and more modern structures. Following World War II, as much of the rescue work was taken over by aircraft, most of the stations were decommissioned. This one, at Kitty Hawk, is now a private residence.

In recent years artists have converged on the Outer Banks, and art classes are held regularly throughout the summer season. Many of Aycock's photographs have been in demand by artists who reproduced the photographic scenes with paint or crayon. This one of the shrimping fleet tied up at the harbor in Stumpy Point has been especially popular.

The guitar pickers and folk singers were photographed by Aycock to publicize The Circus Tent, a popular summer attraction at Kill Devil Hills sponsored by the Dare Ministerial Association.

Summer tourists find an extra bonus on their Outer Banks vacations: watching commercial fishermen unload and sort their catches at dockside.

The return of the charter fleet at Oregon Inlet each afternoon invariably attracts onlookers. Shown is a blue marlin, one of thousands that have been taken by anglers since World War II from Oregon Inlet and Hatteras based cruisers. Aycock was especially pleased with this one, for the captain (with cap on right) is his son Billy Brown, and the mate (holding the line at left) is his grandson Charley Brown.

Seven campgrounds are maintained by the National Park Service in the Cape Hatteras Seashore, and numerous private camping facilities have been opened up and down the Outer Banks in recent years. Aycock took this picture at the Park Service's Oregon Inlet Campground.

BE SURE TO LOOK UP
AYCOCK BROWN

by Joseph Baylor Roberts
retired photographer, *National
Geographic*

Thirty-six years ago I came to North Carolina for the first of a dozen or more *National Geographic* photographic assignments in the colorful and friendly Old North State. That first article, covering the whole state, touched only briefly on the Outer Banks. *The Lost Colony,* Paul Green's innovative outdoor drama of the ill-fated first English settlement, the Wright Brothers National Memorial, plus mention of shipwrecks and pirates did little to tell the story of the northern coastal islands. On their Atlantic side other than strategically placed Life Saving Stations there were two or three seasonal resort hotels and a few vacation homes. Established villages and a few private hunting clubs from Corolla to Ocracoke were tucked in along the Sound side. Except for Manteo, Dare County seat on Roanoke Island, an outsider, unless he was there for hunting or fishing, saw very little of the real people who populated that almost remote region.

In Raleigh, Bill Sharpe, who was the oracle of visiting news gatherers at that time, advised, "When you get to Morehead City and Beaufort be sure to look up Aycock Brown. He's a knowledgeable young reporter-photographer and can be very helpful." For once Bill was on the conservative side. Aycock turned out to be a bundle of energy, a fountain of ideas, and a good influence along the Carolina coast from Kitty Hawk to Wilmington. Ever since we have been mutual admirers and good friends.

About fifteen years and one war later the *Geographic* scheduled an Outer Banks Holiday story. It was my good fortune to have that photographic assignment and better still to find on arrival that the new Dare County Tourist Bureau was Aycock Brown. Where previously a camera seemed an intrusion in the small villages, all had changed. Aycock was so well known and well liked, his name was all the introduction necessary for a friendly reception and often much-needed help. Tourism had come to the Outer Banks and with it prosperity for the waterman and the businessman alike. New modern hotels and motels were spaced between shopping and restaurant areas. Fine, solidly-built, private homes had multiplied by the hundreds. A National Seashore Recreational Area was established by the National Park Service for the preservation and development of large unimproved sections of the island all the way to Hatteras.

Aycock Brown is a man of many talents. Business and civic leaders surely must have used his effective promotional ideas to bring about such notable progress. The December 17th anniversary of man's first flight in 1903 is observed annually, always with Aycock somewhere in the background of arrangements. His daylight photo dress rehearsal of the *Lost Colony* cast yearly brings photographers from far and wide to Fort Raleigh's Outdoor Theatre.

In addition to his ability for handling news and promotion, Aycock possesses a very rare quality which perhaps only another photographer would recognize. He has an inherent instinct about photography, about pictures, which makes him a joy to work with. Looking back over that old issue of the *Geographic* brings happy memories. I count twenty-three out of thirty-four illustrations which are a direct result of his help or suggestions. Altogether we made hundreds of possible pictures as we traveled from Corolla to Ocracoke during the five or six weeks' assignment. Good subjects seemed to appear wherever we roamed, such as the old Whale Head Bridge framing Currituck Light, for instance, and the live oak-shaded little house near Salvo built from shipwreck salvage even to its interior wood paneling from a long forgotten ship's grand saloon.

It wasn't work all the time. Aycock and I were often sidetracked to his comfortable home in Manteo for excellent coffee always ready and waiting to be served by his interested and cooperative wife, Esther. Brantley, their first son, was at sea, later becoming an airline pilot. Younger son Billy, in high school, was helpful. He knew where an osprey nest could be pictured, and Stormy Gale, youngest of the family, when posing with a neighbor's colorful doll collection, made a very pretty model.

I gave up active photography in 1960 for a desk job at the *Geographic*, just a few years before retirement, so I am recalling a memorable assignment of nearly twenty years ago. Since then younger *Geographic* men have pictured the Outer Banks, all with the same enthusiasm I always felt. They too sing high praises for Aycock Brown.

In recent years, because of the demand for prints of his photographs, Aycock has devised a filing system which enables him to locate prints, negatives, and captions. The filing system for the earlier ones is something else again, but for this chapter Aycock finally produced for the editor a representative sampling of oldies. In this picture an Outer Banks fisherman, his name long forgotten, was hard at work mending his fish net between hauls, oblivious to Aycock and his camera.

When J. F. Turner moved to Wanchese he lived first in a boat, and later built a house over the boat, with the bow protruding. This was an oddity which attracted tourists and photographers. A picture of Turner and his boathouse was featured in one of the *National Geographic Magazine* articles mentioned by Joe Baylor Roberts.

Andy Griffith was one of many actors whose early stage careers got a boost with a part in *The Lost Colony*. For years Griffith has owned a home on Roanoke Island. In this picture, taken in the early 1950s, Sir Walter Raleigh (Griffith) hands a pipe filled with tobacco from the New World to Queen Elizabeth (Lillian Prince) while a page girl (Sylvia Cox) looks on.

For many years the late Scotty Gibson, left, operated the Atlantic View, the only hotel at Hatteras, while the late Stanley Wahab, right, was the owner of the hotel at Ocracoke. Wahab, an Ocracoke native who left home to launch a successful business career in the Baltimore area, returned to Ocracoke, where he was involved in a variety of ventures all designed to make Ocracoke a more enjoyable place in which to live, or to visit.

One of Aycock Brown's first successful promotional efforts in Dare County was publicizing the Carolinian Hotel's annual fox hunts. In this picture taken in the early 1960s, Reverend Edwin T. Williams, Rector of the Holy Trinity Episcopal Church, Hertford, North Carolina, stands on the tail gate of a pickup truck as he conducts "the blessing of the hounds," traditional opening ceremony for the fox hunts.

Even when Portsmouth was a thriving community, delivering the mail involved a complicated process. Mailman Carl Dixon, shown here, would pole his skiff out to the channel each day to meet the mail boat from Atlantic. Then, when he reached shore, he would transfer the mail bags to his wheelbarrow for the trip across the marsh to the Post Office.

Mother Vineyard on the north end of Roanoke Island, said to have been the original scuppernong grape vine in this country, once covered more than an acre. Now only the large old mother vine remains, but when Aycock took this picture in the late 1940s the Mother Vineyard Winery was flourishing. The late Tull Lennon sits in the doorway to the winery, as a laborer approaches in a horsedrawn cart filled with scuppernongs.

In his personal diary Orville Wright reported that there were five witnesses when he and his brother Wilbur made their first successful flights December 17, 1903: three crewmen from the nearby Kill Devil Hills Life-saving Station who assisted them, a Manteo merchant, and a young boy, Johnny Moore of Nags Head, who happened to show up when the preparations were being made that morning and stayed around to see what the excitment was all about. This was one of the last pictures of John Moore, the last surviving witness to man's first successful flight.

A highlight of the bus trip down the banks was the ferry trip across Oregon Inlet before the construction of the Herbert C. Bonner Bridge.

Mashoes, on the Dare County mainland, once a thriving
fishing community, was fast becoming a ghost town
when Aycock took this picture in 1970.

When escorting visiting editors and writers around the
Outer Banks in the days before easy access over modern
roads and bridges, Aycock invariably gave them a first
hand look at the United States Coast Guard in action at
one of the many lifeboat stations along the coast. Here
the late Bill Sharpe, for many years editor of *The State
Magazine,* helps the Chicamacomico Station crew move
the boat carriage.

Longtime "Keeper" (Non-Commissioned Officer In Charge) of the Chicamacomico Station was the late "Captain" Levene Midgett. He and his pet Chesapeake Retriever posed for Aycock with the station in the background and the dog guarding the Lyle Gun.

The annals of the United States Lifesaving Service, and its successor the United States Coast Guard, contain numerous accounts of acts of extreme heroism by men of the Outer Banks, and a surprisingly large number of them were Midgett's. One of the most famous was Rasmus S. Midgett, who discovered the sailing vessel *Priscilla* ashore while on beach patrol in 1899, and is credited with single-handedly saving the entire crew of ten. Aycock took this picture of his two proud sons holding the Gold Lifesaving medal awarded Rasmus for his heroic deed.

Aycock's caption for this 1962 picture reads as follows: "COAST CATS ORIGINATED FROM SHIP-WRECKED ANCESTORS—Most of the coastal cats originated from animals which originally were cast ashore from wrecked ships. This is especially true of those which have strains of Persian, or Maltese. Most hardy of the kittens are the bluish-gray Maltese species like the pet of Mrs. Ruth Best of Stumpy Point, who is shown in photo. A unique feature of the Outer Banks and coastal Maltesers is the fact they have seven toes instead of five."

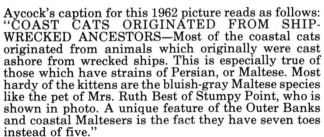

Nags Head had become a famous "watering place" or summer resort prior to the Civil War, but until the 1930s the summer cottages were mostly located on the soundside, with only a handful on the ocean beach. By the late 1940s, when this picture was taken at Kill Devil Hills, the resort had spread north along the oceanfront with several hundred modern summer "cottages" in evidence.

Before the roads were paved on the Outer Banks it was
necessary to follow in sandy tracks made by other cars,
with tires deflated. Even with experienced drivers it was
frequently necessary for all hands to get out and push.

The skeleton of a live oak tree stands lonely sentinel over the Midgett family graveyard at Waves in this early photograph by Aycock Brown.

Three well known Roanoke Island personages were pictured together as they rode in an oxcart in a parade during the commemoration of Dare County's eightieth birthday in 1950. George Harvey Midgett, owner of the ox and cart, was at the controls; Captain Jeff Hayman and Judge Washington Baum were the passengers. Midgett, nearing his one hundredth birthday, was the only one of the trio still alive in 1976.

Scenes like this were once common along the Outer Banks. The one room shacks, usually constructed of boards found washed up on the beach, were used by fishing crews when seining on the beach. Aycock posed his daughter Gale beside the shack one sunny afternoon.

Joe Baylor Roberts of *National Geographic Magazine* and Aycock set up this picture of two little boys standing on a bridge at Whalehead Club, Corolla, with Currituck Beach lighthouse framed beneath. This black and white picture by Aycock was widely printed in the early 1950s. The companion picture, in color, was published in *National Geographic Magazine*.

KNOW AYCOCK BROWN?
I LOVE HIM!

by John E. Blizzard
general manager, *Conquistador* outdoor
drama, Arkansas

If anyone should ever ask me if I know Aycock Brown I would have to say no.

I don't just know Aycock. I love him.

And I love the way he does things. Like the time he told me why his stories got published in the *Virginian-Pilot* and mine didn't. Like the time he gave me a gaudy red plaid bow tie that could never match anything I would ever wear just because he saw it and liked it. Like the time we shared a cup of coffee, just us, and we talked about his half-a-century-old, and my still-green, secrets of the public relations agent.

There isn't any real trick behind getting stories published in the *Virginian-Pilot*. An Aycock Brown byline will do it every time.

So a gaudy red bow tie doesn't match any jacket, shirt, hat, belt, socks, suit, or shoes you own; Aycock always gets away with wearing the tie no one else could ever find, or would buy if they could, and somehow receives a compliment on his choice.

Whether green or half-a-century-old, Aycock contends, basics for becoming a good public relations agent are still the same—the greatest quality he can have is the ability to find someone else to do the work for him. And although Aycock swears by this philosophy, somehow that someone else always seems to resemble Aycock.

The picture favors one developed at five a.m. in an over-crowded darkroom tucked away in a two-story white residence on Sir Walter Street...the story sounds a lot like it was written by the midnight oil from the former sun porch at the Manteo Community Building...and, without a doubt, there is a tagline on the envelope saying "covering the waterfront"...that's probably because somehow, somewhere in his busy schedule, Aycock Brown has found the time to spend eighteen hours between his at-home darkroom and downtown office to get the job done himself.

That someone else who Aycock Brown finds to do the work for him is just another of the well-known personalities emerging from an ever-faithful, never-tiring conviction within himself.

Some have called him workaholic. Some have called him fool. Modestly, Aycock probably would choose the latter and go on to explain, as he always seems to find the time to do.

What it was that made Aycock Brown tackle the job of putting the Outer Banks of North Carolina on the map I'll never know. And I'm not sure Aycock himself can put it into words. But he, and I, and all the world alike are thankful that he did.

I consider myself one of the fortunate ones who has had a chance to share many things with Aycock. Cups of coffee, deadlines, frustrations, and the only paper cutter in the county—these memories I cherish.

For three exciting, educational years I was separated from Aycock by only a single-panel door between the offices of the public relations director of *The Lost Colony* outdoor drama and the director of the Dare County Tourist Bureau. It didn't take me long to realize that on the other side of that door was a living legend—a dry wit, a brilliant craft, and a knowledge of practically every decent journalist in the nation. I was sitting next to a goldmine and I wanted to see every shining stone in it.

I am not sure why Aycock took to me like he did, but I guess I would have resigned from my post and sheepishly crawled away with my tail between my legs had he not. He opened his heart and his files to me, and I dug in.

One look at Aycock's files, if they can be called anything other than disheveled piles, shows that he doesn't believe in throwing anything away. Thirty-year-old telephone directories, yellowed newspaper clippings, and an assortment of all-empty liquor containers that would put any bottle collector to shame are some of the most obvious accumulations. And behind every item is a story, probably a story that Aycock has a clipping about to show its merit.

As well as saving things, Aycock saves ideas. It's like he stores them up and waits until the right time to release them, and you might well know the releases will be timely.

In his diligence to sell the Outer Banks, however, Aycock's wit never dies. He meets the anxious vacationer at the Tourist Bureau with the same zeal that he beats out a cutline for his famous fishing photographs, and he greets his office staff and friends with a loving piece of candy at least once a day.

He used to bounce into my office at the end of every afternoon to cut out the light over his desk from a central control panel we shared; inevitably he would be whistling a tune or recalling a humorous story from the time when he had fretted over the same deadlines I was facing that particular time.

It amazes me to pause and consider the brilliant craft he has developed and consider the multitude of people he has been able to reach through its evolution. His off-the-cuff knowledge of the country's major media representatives exemplifies his persistence.

Of all the rewards and honors I should ever receive, I shall always gleam on remembering the first time Aycock asked me to write a cutline for one of his photographs. For some reason that seemed as important to me as an assignment from the managing editor of the *New York Times*.

On looking back at the three years Aycock and I shared that light switch, I have only one regret. I wish I had found time to write more cutlines for his fish pictures.

During my stay at "Aycock Brown's Outer Banks" I received probably the greatest compliment I could ever imagine. I had borrowed Aycock's camera equipment-filled car to run an errand downtown and decided to stop in at the local diner for a quick cup of coffee. As I pulled to the sidewalk parking space I heard someone call out "Aycock," obviously in recognition of his name-plated car. When I stepped out and the caller realized it was me instead of Aycock he remarked "Well, I guess it's Aycock, Junior." I thanked him, then I thanked God for my esteemed relationship with the "Outer Banks' Oyster" as I proudly marched into the restaurant.

I drove back to my office with a glowing smile and a new respect. Know Aycock Brown, I thought. I love him.

Paul Green's *The Lost Colony,* an experiment in outdoor
theatre which he calls a symphonic drama, was presented in a natural amphitheatre at Fort Raleigh in
1937 to mark the 350th anniversary of the first attempt
at English settlement in America. Surprisingly well received, it was presented again in 1938, and nearly forty
years later is drawing larger crowds than ever. Aycock
Brown has handled publicity for the production for
more than a quarter century. Aycock's aerial photograph of Waterside Theatre has been printed in numerous publications.

A late afternoon shot of the main stage of Waterside
Theatre, where *The Lost Colony* is presented six nights
weekly each summer.

When Aycock began publicizing *The Lost Colony* visitors entered Fort Raleigh between these block-houses, constructed in the 1930s with WPA labor as part of a "reconstruction" of the sixteenth century "Cittie of Ralegh in Virginia." The log-type structures have since been removed and a new entrance constructed.

The Lindsay Warren Visitor Center at Fort Raleigh is named for Lindsay C. Warren, congressional leader who represented the Outer Banks district in the House of Representatives for many years, and later became Comptroller General of the United States.

Special ceremonies frequently are held on the stage of Waterside Theatre during intermission of *The Lost Colony*. At this one in 1962, the dignitaries were preparing to bury a strongbox containing mementos of the day. From left: Dare County Representative Keith Fearing, author Paul Green, Congressman Herbert C. Bonner, Governor Terry Sanford, Secretary of the Interior Stuart Udall, *Lost Colony* producer Mrs. Emma Neal Morrison, National Park Service Director Conrad Wirth, and Waterside Theatre builder Albert Bell.

Mabel Evans Jones of Roanoke Island, longtime member of *The Lost Colony* cast and producer of a moving picture about the lost colony in the 1920s, was given the honor of lighting the "birthday" candles on the occasion of the thousandth performance of Paul Green's drama. From left: veteran *Lost Colony* costumer Irene Rains, Mrs. Mattie Melson, Mrs. Jones, and Marjalene Thomas, a member of the cast since 1938.

The masts and rigging of *The Lost Colony's* realistic looking ship, which moves on tracks behind the stage.

Rehearsals occupy much of the time of members of the cast of *The Lost Colony,* even those who have been with the show for many years, such as Cora Mae Basnight of Manteo, who plays the part of Agona.

When disaster struck Waterside Theatre in the form of Hurricane Donna just after the end of the 1960 season, his editor friends could still count on Aycock providing photographic coverage. This view shows the devastation of a building backstage.

For a number of years the director of *The Lost Colony* has been Joe Layton, who has many New York and Hollywood credits for stage, screen, and television productions. Here Layton paints authentic designs on the legs of Indian maidens prior to the start of a performance.

Charles Smith, who played the part of the Indian chief Manteo during the early 1960s, was being photographed by a comely picture taker during dress rehearsal when Aycock got this picture of them both.

Robert Armstrong, an Alabama native who has appeared as a featured character actor in numerous movies and television productions in recent years, played the male lead of John Borden in the 1947 production of *The Lost Colony*.

Year after year the newspapers publish pictures of this type provided by Aycock. His caption for this one reads: "One of the colorful and dazzling early scenes in Joe Layton's production of Paul Green's *The Lost Colony,* presented throughout the summer at Waterside Theatre on Roanoke Island."

The Indian dances are always a highlight of *The Lost Colony* for spectators of all ages, and especially for photographers. In the late 1940s Aycock took this picture of John Lehman as Uppowoc, the Indian medicine man, performing the Corn Harvest Dance surrounded by Indian maidens.

Virginia Dare was the first child born of English parentage in the New World (August 18, 1587) and the first child baptized in America (August 24, 1587). Photographs of the dramatization of these events in *The Lost Colony* have always proved popular with the nation's editors. The mother, Eleanor Dare, comforts the child and colonists gather for the baptism in the chapel on the main stage of Waterside Theatre.

Leading actors in *The Lost Colony* assemble for a group publicity picture in the early 1970s.

The final scene of *The Lost Colony* shows the small band of men and women marching off into the wilderness, and oblivion. This was always a favorite scene for visiting photographers at the annual dress rehearsals.

The normal lighting in Waterside Theatre is not adequate for pictures showing both the stage and the audience. So when *National Geographic* photographer Emory Kristoff trucked in special lighting equipment from Washington for this 1968 performance, Aycock took advantage of the opportunity to get some pictures of his own.

THERE IT IS IN LIVING COLOR ON MAGAZINE RACKS IN PORTLAND, PEORIA, AND PITTSBURGH

by Gilbert Love
retired travel columnist, *Pittsburgh Press*

Rain had lashed the Outer Banks all night. At dawn I was wakened by the telephone in my room at the Carolinian Hotel, Nags Head.

The caller was Aycock Brown. "If you still want to go to Hatteras today I'll take you," he said. "You might get stuck. Anyway, there are some things I want to show you."

He picked me up and we went splashing southward over often-flooded roads, hurrying to make the Oregon Inlet ferry, as one frequently did in the days before the big bridge. As we rocked across the inlet, Aycock recited tales of sports events that had to be canceled, with audiences in their seats, because one team was on a ferry that got hung up on a shifting sand bar.

The weather cleared somewhat while we were driving the long, lonely road through Pea Island National Wildlife Refuge. We stopped to inspect the remains of a wrecked ship; paused to photograph the now-useless bridge at New Inlet, sealed again by the sea.

At Rodanthe, Aycock chuckled over tales of the Old Christmas celebration held there each January 5. He was much more serious in telling about the lifesaving stations on this coast and the crewmen they had rescued after ships were torpedoed, often within sight of persons on shore.

In Buxton we listened for a time to an elderly gentleman who told some fairly wild stories about his adventures at sea. In Hatteras, Aycock steered me to back yards where grapefruit and orange trees were growing.

Somewhere in that area we walked through a big house whose first floor was almost entirely devoted to pieces of driftwood picked up by the lady of the house because of some resemblance to Bible characters or situations.

When we got back to Nags Head I had material for half a dozen columns in *The Pittsburgh Press*. I'm sure they did no harm to the cause of tourism on the Outer Banks.

Aycock Brown is one of the most effective publicists I know. He doesn't push, or try to "sell" stories of doubtful value, but helps you get material you want and occasionally comes up with an idea you can use.

He's genuinely friendly, too. After a while you contact him more as an informed friend than a publicity man. He has been on the Banks a long time and seems almost their proprietor.

For one reason or another, he has obtained more publicity for the Outer Banks than even this delightful region would ordinarily get. It's difficult to think of a national magazine, with any leaning toward travel, that hasn't featured the Banks at least once.

Aycock conducts their writers and photographers through his domain and, within a few months, there it is in living color on magazine racks in Portland, Peoria, and Pittsburgh. I can testify, from experience with my own articles, that people respond in droves to such stimuli.

One of the headquarters for the ferry boat operation was this building on the north side of Oregon Inlet. When automobiles driving up the beach from the lower banks reached the south side of the inlet they would raise a flag on a high pole to signal Captain Tillett to come across and pick them up. Captain Tillett, an avid fisherman, is standing, center, in white in this photograph, with his surf rod at the ready.

The late Toby Tillett pioneered ferry service across Oregon Inlet, providing vehicular access to and from Hatteras Island. For nearly thirty years, beginning in the mid-1920s, Captain Tillett continued to improve his service with larger and better equipped vessels. This early Tillett ferry, probably the *New Inlet,* carried a maximum of five automobiles when properly loaded on deck.

For many years this larger ferryboat, the *Barcelona,* carried vehicles and passengers back and forth across Oregon Inlet. This early aerial photograph by Aycock shows the *Barcelona* underway with five vehicles on board, each of which was charged a modest toll by Captain Toby Tillett for the one-way trip.

The early Tillett ferries were designed to head into shore at the most likely spot on any given day and drop a gangplank for the cars and passengers to come aboard. The north side ferry landing, wherever it happened to be, was always a popular spot for fishermen and tourists. This picture was taken in the 1940s.

Captain Tillett's locally-built wooden-hulled ferries were replaced by the state of North Carolina with converted landing craft such as the *Governor Umstead,* shown here.

In the 1950s the State Highway Department took over the Oregon Inlet ferry operation, removing the tolls and purchasing Captain Toby Tillett's ferries, which remained in service until larger vessels could be acquired. There still was no road at the south side of Oregon Inlet, and more often than not unsuspecting drivers would get stuck before passing out of sight of the ferry landing.

With the completion of North Carolina State Highway 12 the length of Hatteras Island, tourists by the thousands were drawn to the free ferry ride across Oregon Inlet, and the state purchased a fleet of larger ferries designed for crossing the shallow inlet. Because the channels were narrow the ferries passed at close range, giving Aycock an opportunity to get this close-up shot of the *Lindsay Warren* loaded to the gunnels.

This long line of cars waiting for the ferries to transport them across Oregon Inlet to Nags Head and the mainland was photographed on the newly completed state road at the north tip of Hatteras Island.

Camera always at the ready, Aycock took this shot of
the trawler fleet as he crossed Oregon Inlet on the state
ferry.

At long last Oregon Inlet was bridged in the early 1960s, bringing joy to those whose business called for frequent trips to and from Hatteras Island, but regret for nostalgia buffs for whom the ferry trip had been an experience long remembered.

Oregon Inlet Coast Guard Station, on the south side of
the inlet, is one of the few lifeboat stations on the Outer
Banks which is still in service.

At Rodanthe, some twelve miles south of Oregon Inlet,
the decommissioned Chicamacomico station has long
been considered as the site for a museum depicting the
activities of the United States Lifesaving Service and
the United States Coast Guard within the area com-
prising the present day Cape Hatteras National
Seashore.

Rodanthe is the site of the "Old Christmas" celebration, held annually on the fifth of January. A feature of the affair, which attracts Aycock Brown and numerous other photographers, is the appearance of the legendary "Old Buck," which undergoes changes each time a new "Keeper" is selected. John Herbert of Rodanthe poses for Aycock with his version of "Old Buck."

Spectators crowd around "Old Buck" and his keeper during an "Old Christmas" celebration at Rodanthe.

Portsmouth, once the largest community on the Outer Banks, was in the process of becoming a "ghost town" when Aycock returned to take this picture of the former post office and general store. Accompanying the photographer were Summers Spencer and Aycock's son Brantley A. Brown, who are seated on the porch.

A traditional part of special events on Hatteras Island
is a demonstration by the United States Coast Guard.
In this instance surfmen from the old Chicamacomico
station were preparing to launch their surfboat through
the breakers.

The British Cemetery at Ocracoke, where residents of the Outer Banks community buried British sailors whose bodies washed ashore after a World War II sinking, is a must for island visitors. Aycock escorted a *National Geographic* crew to Ocracoke, and took this picture of writer William Ellis reading the inscription on the cemetery fence.

This huge slab of stone marks the grave at Portsmouth of John Wallace, "Governor of Shell Castle," who died in 1810. Shell Castle was an island or "rock" of oyster shells in Pamlico Sound just back of Ocracoke Inlet, on which Wallace built an extensive trading center and docks for transhipping cargo from oceangoing vessels to smaller craft which could navigate the shallow sound waters.

I FOUND MY ACCESS
TO THE OUTER BANKS

by Bruce Roberts
author/photographer, Charlotte, North
Carolina

Since the death of the Wright brothers, Aycock Brown is the greatest living institution in the vicinity of Kitty Hawk.

I first met him back in the late fifties in the inner sanctum of the Dare County Tourist Bureau. The walls of his office were covered with photographs of girls and fish. The furniture was invisible, hidden under piles of papers, news clippings, and contact sheets. It was as if someone had compressed the entire newsroom of *The Charlotte Observer* into one small room. On the wall was a phone which looked as if it had been installed the day after the Wright flight.

Here I found my access to the Outer Banks. There was nothing that existed on the Banks that Aycock Brown could not find, dig up or direct you to—or, if one was uncertain as to directions, he'd close the door of his office and get into his car—you could always tell which one was his because the license read "Aycock" on the back—and he would lead you to the spot you wanted to go.

I recall the first trip I made to the Outer Banks in the middle of February. Some crazy editor in New York wanted pictures of the Graveyard of the Atlantic, shipwrecks and wreckage. It took Aycock about five minutes on the phone to locate a ship's nameplate—it turned out to be the ferryboat *New York* which had gone down in a storm while being towed toward New Orleans to be put into service again.

Aycock and I placed the nameplate in the foam at the water's edge and while he made sure it didn't wash out to sea again, I photographed it as if it had just arrived on the beach in a storm.

My next trip in the middle of February, Aycock talked his grandson into leap frogging over the ribs of the wreck of the *Laura Barnes* with a fishing pole in hand. Then he located a beach buggy for me to get a shot of Hatteras Light from the point. In three or four days, thanks to Aycock, I had a great photo essay for the editor in New York.

The next time I saw Aycock I needed to borrow the entire cast of *The Lost Colony* for a picture for a North Carolina travel ad. It might have been a problem for anyone else, but by the next day at three o'clock, Aycock had turned out some sixty persons—all in full costume—at the water's edge for my picture. In the morning he had gotten my check cashed for me so I could pay each of the people a small amount for their trouble.

It was Aycock that could take a northeastern storm and put a label on it like the "Ash Wednesday Storm" so that from that day on every editor was comparing hurricane damage to the great "Ash Wednesday Storm." It was Aycock who could tell you those who had really known the Wright brothers, who could find a girl or a family or a kid to pose for pictures on the beach in the middle of winter.

Several years passed before I ever received an assignment to photograph the Outer Banks in summer. In February the New York editors begin to think about their summer issues. I must have shot a summer feature in February for five years before I ever saw how the Banks looked in the summer with tourists. It was Aycock who made it all possible. Without his providing props and models, without his knowledge of locations—where the sun would set and where the snow geese would be—I could never have shot summer features in February.

After some twenty years, it seems impossible to think of the Outer Banks without Aycock in the inner recesses of the Dare County Tourist Bureau.

If some Harvard public relations type arrives to take his place, the Outer Banks may be doomed to obscurity, perhaps even left off the maps. But even if that happens there are still thousands of people who will continue to come to the Outer Banks because Aycock Brown was there.

When adversity hits the Outer Banks Aycock, unlike most publicists, keeps right on clicking his camera shutter. And, as Bruce Roberts reports, it was Aycock who gave the name "Ash Wednesday Storm" to the disaster which struck the east coast March 7, 1962, "so that from that day on every editor was comparing hurricane damage to the great 'Ash Wednesday Storm.'"

There was damage aplenty, from South Carolina to New England, and on Aycock's beloved Outer Banks no less than anywhere else, as his pictures attest. This was Highway 158 Business in Kitty Hawk, after the storm tides had subsided.

With the highway buried under three feet of sand, newsman Laverne Watson takes a rest before following
Aycock down the beach.

The next day highway department graders and
bulldozers had made a first effort at clearing a track
for vehicles to follow.

Many cottages were badly damaged by the storm.

The Oregon Inlet Fishing Center was temporarily out of business.

Along the beachfront a fishing pier withstood the on-slaught of the sea, but oceanside cottages were less fortunate.

After the storm, with the area under martial law, property owners waited their turn to be escorted by special deputies to their cottage sites.

And nothing was left of this oceanfront store except the cash register.

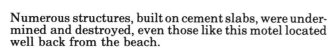

Numerous structures, built on cement slabs, were undermined and destroyed, even those like this motel located well back from the beach.

Buildings far removed from the ocean were destroyed when the surging waters, driven by near hurricane force northeasterly winds, formed a river leading to the sound.

Near Buxton a large bulldozer disappeared, and is yet to be found, and except for its elevated bucket and the tip of its boom this dragline might have suffered a similar fate.

Kitty Hawk Pier

Kill Devil Hills

Before the storm waters had subsided Aycock took to the air to record the destruction.

Nags Head Coast Guard Station

The Nags Head Coast Guard Station, already decommissioned, was now readied for extinction.

The Nags Head Soundside Road had become a raging torrent as impounded water sought an outlet to the sound.

Nags Head Beach

Though no vessels were reported lost on the Outer Banks as a result of the "Ash Wednesday Storm," at other times the "Graveyard of the Atlantic" has taken a heavy toll. This is the World War II ship *Betelguese,* which drifted ashore between Waves and Salvo on January 17, 1976. Salvors worked for nearly two months before freeing the vessel.

When Aycock took this picture on Ocracoke in the 1950s, this was all that remained of the *Carroll A Deering,* the famed "Ghostship of Diamond Shoals" which was discovered by lifesavers hard aground, with sails set, but no sign of her crew.

Long after the excitement is over, the skeletons of wrecked vessels on the Outer Banks attract spectators, surf fishermen—and photographers.

The remains of old sailing vessels periodically are uncovered when the shifting sands erode.

The fishing trawler *Miss Pamlico* was in serious trouble when Aycock took this picture. Finally beaten to pieces on the Oregon Inlet shoals, she became a total loss.

The trawler *Ralph Eugene* was left high and dry on the beach after drifting ashore at Salvo in a mid-1950s storm.

Being towed south, this was one of two surplus LST's which broke loose off the Outer Banks in a severe storm in the early 1950s and came to a final resting place on the beach at Chicamacomico.

The *Eastern I,* a stripped down World War II Liberty Ship, drifted ashore at Southern Shores in the late 1960s, but was finally refloated.

THERE ARE TWO AYCOCKS, DON'T YOU SEE

by Jack Aulis
columnist, *The News & Observer,*
Raleigh, North Carolina

I have seen two Aycock Browns over the past twenty-five years, both unique. First we had the peacock-bright, open-collar, sports-shirt Aycock. Then there was the latter-day, necktie-wearing Aycock.

In either plumage he has done more to make the Dare Coast Outer Banks known than any other man, with the possible exception of Wilbur and Orville Wright. Who were two men, don't you see.

"Don't you see," with no question mark at the end, is Aycock Brown's favorite expression. It doesn't mean anything. It's just a thing he likes to say, don't you see.

During the era of the first Aycock Brown, you could find him in any crowd. You just looked for the most flaming sports shirt around, and for a floppy-brimmed plantation hat. Aycock looked like a skinny, blue-eyed peacock with cameras draped all over it.

He once told me he had about fifty such sports shirts. "Most of them are what I guess you'd have to call gaudy. They've got trees and flowers and things like that on them," he said.

Gaudy? It was my contention at the time that, properly exploited, Aycock would himself be a prime tourist attraction. If people come from everywhere just to see a snow goose or a left-handed conch shell, imagine the crowds you could attract with a walking, mustachioed camera rack that had been dipped in several colors of phosphorescent paint.

However. In 1975 when I visited Aycock, he was wearing a necktie. And a shirt that was the same, quiet pastel color all over. He had molted.

What happened to all those neon shirts? "I kind of got out of that, don't you see," Aycock said. "I look more like a banker than an Outer Banker, don't I?" He did. Although his socks were lemon yellow.

But he was still Aycock. Still touting Dare County places and Dare County photos and Dare County stories to anyone who would listen. Aycock Brown is a press agent in his heart. No item has ever been too small, no news story too large, for him to handle. Whatever it is, Aycock will think up an angle that will get it printed or filmed or tape-recorded—probably all three.

He got into publicity work almost at the same time he got his first coastal job as a reporter in 1928 on the old *Beaufort* (North Carolina) *News,* a weekly. They built a toll bridge from Morehead City to Atlantic Beach and put up a dance pavilion near the surf. Aycock took on the pavilion as a client.

"They thought I was a helluva press agent, don't you see," he told me, "because one of the first things I did was name that place 'The Pagoda by the Sea.' Well, hell, they didn't know that Kipling had written that a long time ago."

I expect they did know it. But the point is that, even if they did, they would still have thought Aycock was a helluva press agent. Because he was. And is. The change from psychedelic shirts to pastel shirts with necktie has not altered that. He is still Aycock; still unique. And he does, after all, still wear all those cameras and, in summer, a plantation hat.

Aycock has worn a hat every summer since a lengthy photo-taking session in the Elizabethan Gardens one broiling day when he got a touch of sunstroke and fell out of the tree in which he and his cameras had been perching.

Some say he hasn't been the same since. But the truth is he was never the same before, either, don't you see.

Aycock took advantage of two of his favorite photo elements, the beaches of the Outer Banks and a pretty model, and added a pair of sunglasses to produce a widely published picture which might be considered the ultimate in special effects photography for a beach resort publicist. The model was Suzanne Stokes, then a member of the Elizabeth City High School Band.

The Elizabethan Garden, a project of the Garden Clubs of North Carolina, Inc., is located adjacent to Fort Raleigh on the north end of Roanoke Island. In 1952 Garden Club officials and other dignitaries gathered at the site to study plans and inspect the budding project.

Work was well along on the Elizabethan Garden when this 1952 picture was taken.

In early 1953 the Elizabethan Garden was ready for planting.

The completed Elizabethan Garden, featuring the antique eleventh century Pompeian stone fountain with Farnesi coat of arms, is in the center of the sunken gardens.

By the early 1960s the Elizabethan Garden was a reality as dignitaries gathered to hear comments by then Governor Terry Sanford.

One of the many winding trails, this one passing close to a massive oak tree, had been completed when Jeanelle Moore, wife of North Carolina's governor Dan Moore, visited the Elizabethan Garden in the late 1960s.

The proximity of the Elizabethan Garden to Fort
Raleigh and the Waterside Theatre results in frequent
special summertime festivities featuring members of
The Lost Colony cast.

Two views of the gatehouse at the Elizabethan Garden,
one showing the crest of Henry VIII over the doorway,
and the other the Howard fountain in the courtyard.

Aycock took advantage of a rare snowfall to get this picture of the entrance to the Elizabethan Garden.

Roanoke Island native and retired serviceman Louis Midgett, longtime superintendent of the Elizabethan Garden, takes personal pride in the wide variety of flowers and plants available for inspection by visitors.

Tobacco, known to the Indians as "uppowoc," was introduced to England by Raleigh's explorers on their return from Roanoke Island. Thus the Elizabethan Garden features a bed of North Carolina tobacco.

The reflecting pools in the Galleon Esplanade at Nags Head offer opportunities for unusual photographic effects.

Like any experienced photographer, Aycock continues to experiment with special effects, as in this unusual montage. Actually it was a double exposure. The sleeping boy is his son Billy Brown.

Two young girls, framed within the circular outline of a bicycle wheel, result in the kind of picture which catches the fancy of newspaper readers and photo editors alike.

Aycock uses the same technique elsewhere to get this unusual picture of soundside pilings. Waiting until the shadows were exactly vertical and the surface of the water absolutely calm, he produced a picture in which it is almost impossible to determine, on the piling at extreme right for example, which part is the piling above water and which is the reflection.

AN ENDLESS FLOOD
OF PICTURES AND IDEAS

by Woodrow Price
columnist and former managing editor,
The News & Observer, Raleigh, North
Carolina

In 1948, which must have been a vintage year for good things, I started writing a fishing and hunting column called "In the Open" for *The News and Observer.* This was the same year, mind you, that Aycock Brown took to the Dare Coast and began flooding us up-staters with pictures and words about this glorious land.

As the years flowed by since, there have been times when I wondered about the authorship of "In the Open." Assuredly, Aycock has had more in the column than I, although perhaps I put the words on paper. The first catch of the season, the last catch of the season, and almost every catch in between—they've come from him.

Ideas for columns? How easy, when the autumn lights twinkled and the editor rumbled that a deadline approached, to turn to Aycock by telephone and learn that wildfowl were building up in large numbers at Pea Island, or someone had just caught the 198th billfish of the season (off the Dare Coast, that is) or that the striped bass run of school-sized fish was just beginning in Croatan and Albemarle Sounds.

And decorative material for the outdoor page? Pictures of beauty queens with fish, pictures of bigwigs with fish, pictures of just fishermen with fish (all caught on the Dare Coast, mind you)—they've come in an endless flood, swamping the puny flow from other coastal sections, creating the impression that the fishing opportunities in Dare are boundless and unequalled, as surely they must be.

I've never found him when he didn't have a story to tell, not even in the dead of winter. Who else along the coast had thought to keep record of how many blue marlin had been landed this year? Who else knew how many records had fallen that year in the realm of big fish? Who else, at any time of day or night, could find you a salty character bulging with the kind of information on which such columns thrive?

Even sitting across from you at the hotel breakfast table, in the fuzz of early morning, he could continue without apparent effort to feed ideas for columns that, if they couldn't be composed that day, surely could be done in the future. All about the Dare Coast, too.

Ah, yes, in the spring, when the publisher's mind turned to special vacation sections, who but Aycock has always been first with a packet of materials about the wonderful things to be found in his favorite land?

Background? Right out of his mind. Color? A walking index to all conceivable angles. Humor? When necessity demanded, he could provide it himself.

Like the day at Oregon Inlet Fishing Center after he'd posed the happy farmer with a 350-pound blue marlin the farmer had caught that day. "How much for one of those pictures?" the angler asked, touching Aycock on the arm.

"I get three dollars for an eight by ten," Aycock said.

A pause, and then the fisherman asked, "How much for a smaller one."

No pause at all. "I don't make 'em any smaller than that," Aycock replied.

Sale lost. Column gained.

Aycock began writing his outdoors column, "Covering the Waterfront," for upstate newspapers shortly before World War II, and has been flooding the press with fishing pictures ever since. Most of the pictures show people with their catches, but in this very early Dare coast picture the only fish are the junior size one being reeled in by the second girl from the right and another just above water. This picture, taken in the late 1940s, is still being published under the heading "Early Aycock."

Aycock took this picture of his young son Billy K. Brown (left) and friends warily inspecting a huge jewfish caught by commercial fishermen. Son Billy's interest in fish continued as he grew to manhood, and for a number of years he has operated his own charter cruiser out of Oregon Inlet.

By the 1950s Aycock had established connections which resulted in his fish pictures being distributed regularly to hundreds of newspapers by the photo syndicates. The secrets to syndication were attractive subjects, catchy captions, and unusual ways of posing fishermen holding the fish. In this widely published 1959 picture cruiser Captain Billy Baum of Wanchese carried two large bluefish slung over his back.

"Little Boy's Blue" was the caption for this one. Date-lined Hatteras it read: "They've got the blues, but these youngsters are happy rather than sad."

The only caption needed for this one to be published widely was: "Outer Banks Beauty with Channel Bass." There was an added note that she caught the fish in the surf near Hatteras Inlet. The angler is Crystal Davis, a Hatteras resident for several years.

Getting the photo syndicates to distribute pictures of record-breaking fish was a cinch. This was a 1958 picture of Mrs. Jean Browning displaying her 69½ pound channel bass caught in the surf at Buxton, at that time according to Aycock's caption "believed to be the largest of its species ever landed by a lady fisherman."

This one was captioned "Little Boy—Big Fish." Aycock remembers that the boy had a terrible time trying to lift the red snapper as he posed for the picture.

The closest most fishermen ever get to seeing big game fish is in picture form in their local newspapers, and for more than two decades Aycock has been providing the nation's editors with a seemingly endless flow of such pictures. This one, in the days when the Hatteras Marlin Club Tournament was truly an international Blue Marlin Classic, shows members of the Club dePesca of Puerto Rico with their day's catch.

The caption of this syndicated 1959 picture headed "Fisher Folk" was datelined Hatteras, and read: "As evidenced by the whopping catch, fishing really runs in the family of Captain Larry E. Jones. Mrs. Jones reeled in the 157-pound, eight-foot blue marlin at left, while son Larry, Jr., 13, topped Mom with his ten-foot, 284-pound marlin (right). Daughter Rocky stands proudly between the big fish, following an outing at Hatteras, N.C."

When they aren't catching big fish off Hatteras or Oregon Inlet, Aycock searches elsewhere for fishing subjects and if he can't get there himself he usually sends somebody else. Obviously the fish were biting when Ray Couch made this picture at the end of one of the eight ocean piers on the Dare Coast-Outer Banks.

When the drum (channel bass) or bluefish are running, surf fishermen and their beach buggies crowd the point at Cape Hatteras.

This 810-pound blue marlin was caught off Hatteras, June 11, 1962, by Gary Stukes of Morristown, New Jersey, fishing with Captain Bill Foster from the cruiser *Albatross II*. At the time it was the largest ever boated, and remained the world record catch on 130-pound test line for twelve years.

The largest blue marlin ever landed from Atlantic Ocean waters was this 1,142 pounder caught July 26, 1974, off Oregon Inlet by Jack Herrington of Allison Park, Pennsylvania. At the time there were no scales at Oregon Inlet large enough to weigh the huge fish, and it had to be taken to the Hatteras Marlin Club to be weighed in. Posing with the record catch which was made on 130-pound test line are the angler, left, and Captain Harry Baum of Wanchese, from whose charter cruiser *Joe Boy* the catch was made.

These modern day spear fishermen, with their catch of sheepshead speared in the vicinity of one of the numerous Outer Banks shipwrecks in the sixties, had no way of knowing that the photographer, Aycock Brown, was one of the first to publicize their sport. Early practitioners used crude homemade spears and handmade Japanese goggles, and were known as goggle fishermen. Aycock promoted the "World's First Goggle Fishing Tournament" at Cape Lookout in 1939, in which editor David Stick, a pioneer goggler, shared the top prize.

Rita Mizelle of Southern Shores is shown in this 1971 picture holding the 24½ pound bluefish she caught fishing the surf at Nags Head, using 20-pound test line. The catch is still the world's record: the largest of the species ever taken by a distaff angler anywhere. Rita, an avid angler and frequent subject for Aycock's pictures, is also an amateur photographer of note. In recent years, under Aycock's guidance, she has covered numerous newsmaking events for him, providing pictures which brought even more publicity to the Outer Banks.

Women anglers are always popular subjects, especially when their catches are record breakers. When Joyce Payne Bell of Manteo caught this 23-pound, 15-ounce bluefish while trolling from her father's cruiser *Gypsy Angler* in 1970, she set a Women's World Record for bluefish on a 50-pound test line.

Another world record was this 53½ pound channel bass, caught in April 1962 on 12-pound test line in the surf near home by Lucille Herbig of Buxton.

Ray Couch of Buxton is one of the official weight masters on the Outer Banks and thus is in a position to check most of the larger catches in the Cape Hatteras area. Several years ago, while serving as chairman of the Dare County Tourist Bureau, Ray began taking pictures of fish caught in his area, thus saving Aycock a special trip down the banks each time a big one was hauled in. Now Ray produces most of the Hatteras Island pictures distributed by Aycock and the Tourist Bureau. Aycock took this particular shot of Ray (left) checking the 82-pound channel bass caught by Jack Scott of Colonial Heights, Virginia, from the Avon Fishing Pier, November 9, 1970.

Joe Menzacco of Point Harbor has probably caught as many record size bluefish from the surf on the upper coast as any angler in history. Here he holds a near record bluefish caught on 12-pound test line in the surf north of Kitty Hawk in 1970. The catch became a state record in that line test category.

The World's All Tackle record catch for bluefish was made at Hatteras Inlet, January 30, 1972, by James M. Hussey of Tarboro. The fish weighed 31-pounds, 12-ounces and measured forty-seven inches from tip to tip.

Louis Van Miller of Petersburg, Virginia, trolling off Oregon Inlet with Captain Bill Austin aboard the *Pert III*, caught this world's record dolphin in the 80-pound test line category.

The Cape Hatteras area is justifiably famous for the seasonal runs of giant red drum or channel bass, but for years Outer Banks record drum were listed second to one caught at Cape Charles, Virginia. It was fitting that this situation was righted by a resident of Hatteras Island, Elvin Hooper of Salvo, who caught this world record 90-pounder on 30-pound test line, November 7, 1973, from the ocean pier at nearby Rodanthe.

THE "JOHN WHITE"
OF THE OUTER BANKS

by John W. Fox
former general manager, *The Lost Colony*
outdoor drama, Manteo, North Carolina

Governor John White of Sir Walter Raleigh's sixteenth century English colony was the first publicist of Roanoke Island and the Outer Banks. He painted pictures that helped sell Queen Elizabeth and England on the New World as the birthplace of the British Empire.

Since 1948 Aycock Brown has been convincing others—including me—that the sand, surf, sunshine, and solitude of this unexcelled vacationland is "The Goodliest Land Under the Cope of Heaven!"

Paul Green's character Old Tom, in *The Lost Colony* outdoor drama, came from the Devon hills of England "to be made a man of."

Aycock emigrated to eastern North Carolina from upland Happy Valley in Caldwell County to become "a man to be admired" as the Oracle of the Dare Coast. His first assignment was to publicize *The Lost Colony*.

During my six years as general manager of *The Lost Colony*, while occupying an office adjoining Aycock's—with the door between seldom if ever closed—it was my privilege to learn how and why he is a super promoter.

There are, in my opinion, two keys to his success. One is his love for and studied knowledge of the history, lore, people, fishes, birds, flowers, and other attributes of the region. The other is his knack of befriending people and getting them to work with and for him.

It was amazing to see him get a vacationing *National Geographic* photographer, or a George Tames of *The New York Times,* to spend hours in the hot sun helping him take pictures of *Lost Colony* performers in rehearsal at the Waterside Theatre. Even camera experts on assignment usually end up sending him scores of prints or negatives of good pictures unused in their publications.

Some might call him a photojournalist. But, there are better writers and technically, he isn't an outstanding photographer—although some of his pictures are masterpieces. But he doesn't have to be that good because of his helping hand to, and developed friendship with, representatives of newspapers, magazines, and the broadcast media from everywhere.

"Press agentry" and "cheesecake" are terms he isn't reluctant to use in describing most of his work and many of his pictures. His days as a newspaperman were a learning process, from advance men from circuses and show business photographers who taught him to focus on legs and bosoms.

Before I began my stint with *The Lost Colony* in 1963 somebody gave me the names of five or six people to "cultivate" and lean on if I wanted to do well. Aycock, of course, was on the list. Neither he nor the others ever let me down. He, in particular, developed my appreciation and understanding of *The Lost Colony*.

To paraphrase John Borden's speech near the end of the play: "Down through the years let there be some whisper of his name, some devotion to the dream of a good life on the Outer Banks which he helps to perpetuate."

Just as John White, the leader of the 1587 expedition to
Roanoke Island, occupied his spare time by painting
pictures of the flowers, plants, and wildlife he saw there,
so does Aycock Brown seek relaxation by photograph-
ing the same subjects that attracted Governor White.
The first colonists mentioned the sunflowers found on
Roanoke Island, and Aycock has made many pictures of
sunflowers in bloom. In this one he caught a bumblebee
enjoying the nectar of the blossom.

These seed pods of a yucca plant, or bear grass, silhouetted against a Roanoke Island sunset, looked to Aycock like a flock of parakeets or other tiny birds.

During the spring the pleasant odor of magnolia blossoms adds a special fragrance to many yards in the Manteo area.

In the Roanoke Island area this flowering plant is known as Cape Jasmine. Elsewhere the flowers of the sweet smelling plant are prized as gardenias. These blossoms were photographed by Aycock in the Elizabethan Garden near Fort Raleigh on the north end of Roanoke Island.

This closeup in the Elizabethan Garden shows the waxy-looking blossoms of a zebra plant.

Outer Bankers call this blossom the "Joe Bell Flower," crediting the man for whom it is named with introducing the first seeds to the Ocracoke area of the Outer Banks. The Joe Bell Flower, or Gaillardia, now grows in great profusion all along the coast, from Nags Head south to Core Banks.

Mrs. Ron Tillett of Wanchese raised this "starfish flower" in a pot but had to wait years for it to blossom. Aycock reports that "although it looks pretty, it smells bad."

These Night Blooming Cereus were photographed in a roadside ditch on the Outer Banks.

These are lady slippers, which thrive in the wildflower section of the Elizabethan Garden.

When the late Monroe Midgett of Stumpy Point complained to Aycock that beetles were devouring the leaves of a grapevine in his garden this "action photo" resulted.

Terns and other shore birds were nesting on the sandy islands back of the Outer Banks when the Raleigh colonists first visited the area in the 1580s, and John White no doubt had difficulty spotting their eggs amid broken shells on an island rookery, as in this picture by Aycock.

A pair of baby terns, vocal but not yet mobile, nestle beside two unhatched spotted eggs in the sand.

Baby terns seem to be calling mama for help as Aycock moved in for this closeup.

Young shorebirds, too young to fly, form a mass as far as the eye can see on this soundside rookery.

After sneaking up on this mixed flock of wild Canadian Geese and ducks, Aycock got his picture just as they took to flight.

140

An egret, silhouetted against a late afternoon sun, seems to be standing sentinel over the rookery on one of the dredged islands back of Oregon Inlet.

Residents of the Outer Banks have found that wild mallards, both the brightly colored drakes and the dull brownish hens, seem to have less fear of human beings than other waterfowl. As a result many flocks of domesticated mallards can be found in the area, and photographers have little difficulty getting close up pictures.

Pea Island National Wildlife Refuge is a primary winter resting ground for the Greater Snow Geese, and they congregate there in flocks of thousands.

When you get this close to a Great White Heron, both the photographer and subject are "looking at the birdie."

AYCOCK HAS WINGS

by Richard Gonder
public editor, *The Virginian-Pilot,*
Norfolk, Virginia

A hurricane was approaching the Dare County Coast on an early fall afternoon some years ago and, although there was some concern evident, the event also bore trappings of being under the sponsorship of the Dare County Tourist Bureau.

Aycock Brown, the bureau's manager, regards such storms as important tools for spreading The Word about North Carolina's Outer Banks and *The Lost Colony.* Carolina and Virginia newsmen and wire service people, to his delight, never fail to show up in force.

The particular blow—I've forgotten her name—afforded me the opportunity of meeting Aycock for the first time. He was standing in front of the Carolinian Hotel, adequately moored with festoons of photographic equipment, grinning in his special way—upwards rather than sideways—forcing good humor from chin to scalp line.

That Carolina mountain twang was familiar enough through numbers of telephone conversations during which he'd helped me make some deadlines. He already had begun to be something of a coastland legend. For one thing, he had sold an article to the *Saturday Evening Post* and, it was widely rumored, was paid four hundred dollars. That alone made him worthy of great respect and a person it would be easy to get comfortable with.

He had had a little dab of booze and gave immediate directions where others could find it. Showpiece for the occasion was (and has been for all of several hurricane watches I've seen Aycock put on) a Coast Guard helicopter parked on the nearly deserted hotel parking lot.

The Coast Guard, damn them, had been busy advising tourists to get off the beach, and that flying banana may have demonstrated the service's remorse. In any case, Aycock believed it lent some class or drama to the event. It was good for pictures.

The storm fizzled as, thankfully, many of them do. Tourists headed back and the newsmen left the beach. Aycock's job of publicist for Paradise had been fulfilled and convincing where he hoped it would count the most.

It proved to me that he can effectively convert to a tool of his trade almost everything Dare County has to offer. So his name and his product have grown to be recognizable across the land.

143

He has decorated more sand hills and beds of sea oats with more beautiful girls, and has taken more pictures of more fish from more angles with more happy sportsmen than probably anyone in the world. These have been published—thousands upon thousands of them.

So, also, with Aycock's other tools—shipwrecks and sea gulls, sunrises and sunsets, bridges and vineyards and people.

And politicians. There are few things he can make more use of than a governor or a congressman visiting *The Lost Colony*. Not only are they good for picturing people with, but also for introducing people to.

Part of his job is making impressions.

Aycock's ability to be where things are happening has created astonishment among editors. He is like a wraith—in the shadows of Hatteras Light one moment and, within the blink of an eye, up he pops at Oregon Inlet or Kitty Hawk.

It is a marvel that this small world comes up with so many newsworthy events.

He feeds spot news to mainland reporters with the same enthusiasm as he feeds publicity. He plays no favorites in the handling of news. If *The Daily Advance* in Elizabeth City asks for help on a story before *The New York Times, The Daily Advance* will get the information first.

If a reporter is on the beach without a cameraman, usually a roll of Aycock's exposed film is made available.

Understandably, Dare County has good press. The Word continues to get out. That man Brown can be depended upon and is completely trusted. He'll never miss a story.

On a summer Sunday a few years back I went to services in St. Andrews-By-the-Sea Episcopal Church at Nags Head. There—would you believe it—he was, conducting services as a lay reader in the absence of the priest.

That's his secret. Aycock has wings.

"There are few things he can make more use of than a Governor or a Congressman visiting The Lost Colony," says Dick Gonder. In this case it was reversed, and photographer Lawrence Williams posed Aycock with three North Carolina governors; from left: Governor Terry Sanford, Aycock Brown, Governor Luther Hodges, Governor Dan Moore.

Aycock's camera covers a wide variety of subjects. This boat race was held on Shallowbag Bay, Manteo's harbor.

On a sunny summer day bathers crowd the beach in Kill
Devil Hills.

"Hey Mom, look what I got."

Hunting has long been a popular winter sport throughout the Outer Banks area.

The little harbor at Avon, formerly Kinnakeet, has attracted many artists and photographers. Avon is one of seven villages on Hatteras Island.

Artists are drawn also to the larger and often overcrowded harbor at Wanchese.

Aycock's lens caught this time exposure of a storm approaching Waterside Theatre.

Aycock had the main street of Manteo all to himself when he took this picture at the height of hurricane Donna's flooding in 1960.

The main building of the old Hatteras Inlet Coast Guard Station had already toppled overboard as the result of Hurricane Ione when Aycock took this aerial photo. The entire complex subsequently disappeared as natural forces opened a new channel through the inlet.

Jockey's Ridge, now at last a State Park, has been a tourist attraction since pre-Civil War days. Sightseers and hang gliders now share this tallest of east coast sand hills.

Ocracoke Lighthouse, and the old keeper's quarters surrounded by live oaks and cedar, are ever popular photographic subjects.

Over and over again newspaper and magazine editors make hurry up calls to Aycock for a picture of two hundred foot high Cape Hatteras Lighthouse, the tallest lighthouse on the American coast. This is the file photo he usually sends them.

As the sun rises over one of the Outer Banks piers, surf fishermen cast into the calm waters waiting for the first strike of the morning.

Neighborhood stores served as shopping centers, gas stations, banking facilities, election headquarters, and community centers throughout the Outer Banks area before the construction of modern roads and bridges. This was the Zene Perry store in Kitty Hawk, which was built on the site of an earlier store built by his father Dempsey Perry after the Civil War.

These triplets seemed wary about standing on the plaque at Waterside Theatre marking the spot where President Franklin D. Roosevelt sat while viewing the August 17, 1937 performance of *The Lost Colony*.

On one of the Outer Banks meetings of the "Honorary Tar Heels"—prominent editors, photographers, and journalists with special interests in North Carolina—somebody set up this trick shot. It shows the late John Randolph, then outdoor editor of the *New York Times,* reading Aycock's *Dare Coast Outer Banks Travel News* while Aycock examined the front page of the *Times*.

One of the most widely published of Aycock's photographs was this one of a gull landing on a pier at Morehead City in the 1940s, with the bright sun as a backdrop. The picture is still appearing in print.

HE WEARS MANY HATS

by Francis Meekins
editor, *The Coastland Times,* Manteo,
North Carolina

It has been a pleasure and privilege for more than a quarter century in printing and publishing ventures to have felt close to Aycock Brown. Although my father, the late D. Victor Meekins, had worked with Aycock on the *Elizabeth City Independent* many years before I was born, and had contacts with him on many occasions afterward, I did not meet Aycock until the late 1940s when he began work on some special promotional projects in Dare County. At that time he and his family made their home in New Bern, a convenient point to live while working in the emerging tourism and vacation development interests in Carteret County.

Fortunate for the Outer Banks was a meeting of minds, both by Aycock and interested officials, and the Brown family finally settled in Manteo in the 1950s, and Aycock began duties in full-time promotional work for the Dare County Tourist Bureau.

Although his title is manager and news director, he has worn many hats over the years. A day's duties may find him taking photos of notables in the Elizabethan Garden, fishing parties displaying outstanding catches from many of our numerous ports, special events in various other points in the county—enough physical activity to tire even the more youthful—only to find him again working that evening covering the appearance of a dignitary at *The Lost Colony.*

While to some it may seem unlikely that one man can cover so much territory, it actually happens. Many times in the publishing business we have "tips" on some news event, and by the time we get someone assigned to cover it, Aycock has already taken a photograph or has it on schedule. Timely publication of happenings throughout the coastland has been made a great deal easier due to the efforts of Aycock Brown.

His extremely good sources and wide range of contacts throughout the state, nation, and even on the international level has enabled Aycock to get coverage, and the resultant good public relations effects in all publications, television stations and other media interested in the happenings along the Outer Banks.

Our witness to the healthy growth of economy in this area can be attributed to the works of many. Aycock Brown ranks high on the list.

A large percentage of the pictures Aycock has taken on the Outer Banks during the past quarter of a century or so are of people, and especially those he considered close friends. Here is one of his closest friends and supporters, wife Esther, serving yaupon tea at a Nags Head party to Aycock's long-time associate, the late D. Victor Meekins, founder and for many years editor-publisher of *The Coastland Times.*

Sam Jones, another long-time friend and supporter, was photographed by Aycock standing beside the special cemetery at Springers Point on Ocracoke where he had buried his favorite horse, "Ikie D."

Founders of "The Man Will Never Fly Society," whose motto is "Birds fly. Men drink," are shown assembled at one of the meetings of the group, held annually the night before the First Flight ceremonies. Standing, from left: Dr. Ed North and Miriam Rabb; seated, from left: the late Bob Thomas, Jack Aulis, and a fifth character so heavily disguised that nobody seems able to identify him.

Three long-time Outer Banks enthusiasts, left to right: the late Dr. Frank Porter Graham, former president of the University of North Carolina and United States Senator, Mrs. Emma Neal Morrison, who for years headed the Roanoke Island Historical Association, producers of *The Lost Colony,* and Paul Green, author of the longest running outdoor drama in America.

Dick Jordan, then manager of *The Lost Colony,* welcomed Senator and Mrs. Sam Ervin, Jr., to the 935th performance of the drama, July 1959.

Authors of books about the Outer Banks get together at a yaupon tea party in their honor sponsored by Mrs. Lucille Purser Winslow, whose Carolinian Hotel was one of Aycock's first clients on the northern coast. From left: the late Inglis Fletcher, author of *Roanoke Hundred* and other historical novels; David Stick, author of *Graveyard of the Atlantic, The Outer Banks of North Carolina,* and other books about the North Carolina coast; Lucille Purser Winslow; and the late Don Tracy, author of *Carolina Corsair, Roanoke Renegade* and other novels.

The Sons of the Beaches was the name originally given to this popular quartet which performed for a number of years as the Pirate Jamboree Quartet, the Manteo Rotary Club Quartet, and under other names, depending on what they were promoting in the interest of the Outer Banks. Left to right: the late Johnny Long, the late Julian Oneto, Ralph Swain, and Lawrence Swain.

Longtime Dare County Sheriff Frank Cahoon is flanked by two of Dare County's most famous citizens, the late Alpheus W. Drinkwater, left, who operated the telegraph station in Manteo for more than half a century, and the late R. Bruce Etheridge, right, whose service in the North Carolina General Assembly as a representative from Dare County also spanned more than fifty years.

Orville and Wilbur Wright made man's first flights in a heavier than air machine at Kill Devil Hills in 1903, and the late Dave Driskill was the pioneer Outer Banks pilot whose flight record over the Outer Banks according to Aycock's caption for this early picture "rivals that of any goose, duck, or swan to ever spend the winter in coastal sounds." His contribution to modern flight is commemorated at Manteo airport.

One of Aycock's more interesting and versatile subjects was Lucy M. Hooper of Salvo, sports fishing enthusiast, woodcarver, and minister.

George "Georgie Buck" Mann, now a successful Roanoke Island businessman, at one time was one of the area's best known hunting guides.

Charles T. Williams II, Avon community leader turned author, *(The Kinnakeeter,* published in 1975) stands beside a millstone used in one of the old windmills on Hatteras Island.

The late Alpheus W. Drinkwater, famed Manteo telegrapher, giving a civil defense report on an approaching hurricane.

Bootlegging was once big business, especially on the Dare mainland. The late Manteo Police Chief Chester Mitchell, center, Dare County Sheriff Frank Cahoon, right, and Deputy Sheriff Clarence Hassell, located this still in the Kitty Hawk woods in the early 1960s.

Many well-known personalities have moved to the Outer Banks or have plans to, including Charles Kuralt of CBS News, shown filming an "On the Road" sequence at Fort Raleigh during the 1975 Christmas holidays.

Aycock seems to have a knack for getting people to do outlandish things, and appear to enjoy it. Here, under his supervision, the late Governor Luther Hodges displays North Carolina's entry in a Maryland crab derby.

The tables were turned on August 5, 1961, when Aycock became subject rather than photographer. The event was "Aycock Brown Night" at *The Lost Colony,* and the honoree is shown here (left) receiving a gift from the drama's manager Sib Dorton while wife Esther looks on.

Nationally known artist-illustrator Frank Stick, who moved to the Outer Banks in 1929, agreed to have the first and only North Carolina exhibition of his art in 1966, just two months before his death at the age of 82. Aycock shows him here discussing a couple of his water colors at the exhibition in the Carolinian Hotel.

THE CON MAN
OF THE OUTER BANKS

by George Tames
photographer, *The New York Times*

Have you ever met a real live pirate, while walking the dunes, or even seen the ghost of one while night fishing during a dense fog?

How about a direct descendant of Bluebeard? No? Well, neither have I. Wait a minute, I'll take that back. I did meet a son of Bluebeard about twenty-five years ago, but that sly old cutthroat introduced himself to me as Aycock Brown of Manteo and a photographer to boot.

This gracious, charming little man, loaded down with cameras, a pirate? He speaks with a soft North Carolina drawl, with just a hint of Outer Banks, Elizabethan accent, as he asks: "Can you help a fellow photographer with a small problem?"

How was I to know that this small problem was to last for over twenty-five years and that numerous other national photographers were to be drawn in and involved?

Aycock's "little problems," as he explained them, involved publicity pix of the Outer Banks, and although he knew what to shoot and how to do it, he sure would be happy and appreciative if I would just this once help him with this new camera. And so I did. Again, again and again, over the last two decades and more—with problem film, bad lights, and prints.

And, so, we were robbed.

The fact that we gladly submitted to and loved this theft of our talent does not lessen the crime of piracy by Aycock Brown. In other words, he took us.

But we loved it. And we admired him.

Over the years, many of the publicity shots going out under Aycock's name were set up and shot by me and others. I would like to relate only one story to show the technique used by Aycock.

Several years ago, I happened to be in Aycock's office when he placed a small, bluish seashell in my hand.

"Know what this is?" he asked, grinning.

And I could feel it coming. Another small problem.

"You know," he said, "the state of North Carolina has adopted this little seashell, known as the Scotch Bonnet, as the official state shell. And I would like to make some publicity pictures, but I don't rightly know how, and I thought you might have a suggestion to help me."

"Well," I said, "it's very simple. We'll just go out on the beach and find two girls digging shells and when they find a Scotch Bonnet, we'll say: 'Hold it there.' And we'll make the picture."

"There's just one small problem," Aycock said. "It'll make a good shot, but the problem is there's only one shell. And I had to get it from Florida."

"How come?" I asked. "It's the state's official shell, you said."

"Well," he said, "that's not our worry. The state picked it and asked me to publicize it."

"Okay," I said. "Let's go down to the beach and see what we can find."

So we go out on the beach and we spot a pretty girl. I walked up to her and I said: "You are a shell collector."

She said: "Me?"

And I said: "Yes, you. You are a shell collector."

We explained who we were and what we were doing, and we set her up with a collection of shells and had her digging, and lo and behold, up comes this beautiful state shell.

That day we made over fifteen different pictures, using that same shell, of different girls from different parts of the country. And we got very good results for our efforts.

And that, my friends, is the tale of Aycock Brown and his shell game.

A con artist, par excellence.

George Tames' description of the difficulty he and Aycock had in finding Scotch Bonnets—the state of North Carolina's official shell—promoted a search of Aycock's files for a Scotch Bonnet picture to go in this space. After three weeks this is the only one that was turned up. It shows Ray Couch of Buxton, who has taken thousands of Hatteras Island pictures under Aycock's direction in recent years, with a number of the shells found near Cape Hatteras.

One of Aycock's most successful promotional ventures was the Dare Coast Pirates Jamboree, held annually under the sponsorship of the Dare County Tourist Bureau until businessmen tired of growing beards and the purpose—getting the tourist season started in early spring instead of summer—had been accomplished. Here the first Pirate King, Oscar Sanderlin of Kitty Hawk, is confronted by author Don Tracy, while Queen Sarah Alford (Mrs. Robert Owens, and Aycock's assistant for many years) looks on.

An annual feature of the early Jamborees was a beach buggy race on Hatteras Island.

The three-day-long Pirates Jamboree proved a natural for politicians. In this early Jamboree picture, Secretary of State Thad Eure rides a stagecoach with the late A.W. Drinkwater holding the reins, and the late Pat Bayne, that year's king, directing the show.

Each winter crews of Outer Banks pirates took off on promotional tours, appearing on as many as four or five television programs in a single day. Since it was a little early in the season for full grown beards, sometimes they had to fake it—as in this picture showing Aycock in action on a Raleigh television stage.

The Pirates Jamboree theme gave almost limitless opportunities for special poses by photogenic models.

When the Pirates journeyed to Jamestown, Virginia, to promote the 1957 Jamboree, Aycock arranged for one of his pretty models, Dotty Fry, to be put in the stocks by a costumed guard.

The world's largest salt water fish fry—maybe the world's largest any kind of fish fry, but Aycock wasn't sure—was a feature of the annual Jamboree, and attracted large crowds to Cape Hatteras.

Bearded Hatteras Island pirates served as cooks for the fish fry.

Crowds always gathered for the pirate landing. This one
was in Kill Devil Hills.

Even Aycock tried to grow a beard one year, but this
stubble was all he could come up with.

The costume judging for little pirates was a popular feature of the Jamboree.

The climax of the Pirate Jamboree, held each spring during the mid-fifties and early sixties, was the grand Pirate Ball and coronation of the King and Queen. This series shows some of the festivities.

HE CAN SEE ANYBODY, ANYTIME

by Ollie Atkins
Washington editor, *The Saturday
Evening Post*

An old saying within the ranks of professional journalistic photographers says in effect that the world's greatest lensman isn't worth a rap if he can't get in to see his subjects.

This is where Aycock Brown is a master with his camera for he can see anybody, anytime. Furthermore, they are happy to see him. Old Aycock has been doing favors for everyone in the business for all his life.

Nothing sticks in a fellow's mind like a good turn done in the past. Everyone thinks of Aycock in these terms of past favors.

I recall just a couple of years ago having to hurriedly scratch up some graphics for a book project the company was putting together, and some old things I had recalled seeing at the Wright Memorial were involved. It was easy to pick up the phone and have Aycock run the material down and have it on my desk a couple of days later.

His mark is well made on the Outer Banks which he loves. His name is respected in the journalistic profession everywhere.

Old Aycock is a can do - will do *now* kind of fellow, and these are rare people.

Ever since the Wright Memorial was constructed in 1931 aviators have paid homage to the pioneers of flight, circling the memorial or dipping their wings in tribute. This was the view they had in the early 1950s.

Annual celebrations are held at the Wright Brothers Memorial at Kill Devil Hills commemorating the first successful flights by Wilbur and Orville Wright, December 17, 1903. Until a modern visitors center was constructed near the actual site of the first flights on level ground, the December 17 celebrations were held at the base of the Wright Memorial atop the huge sand hill.

Reproductions of the Wright Brothers' original hangar and workshop were constructed in time for the fiftieth anniversary celebration, December 17, 1953.

A reproduction of an early Wright Brothers flying machine was used in a demonstration for visitors at the fiftieth anniversary celebration.

After the new visitor center at the Wright Memorial was completed, Aycock took this aerial shot with the monument centered in the background.

This spot, overlooking Kitty Hawk Bay, is where the Wright Brothers conducted their early gliding experiments before moving down the beach to the larger Kill Devil Hill.

A closeup of the Wright Memorial atop Kill Devil Hill.

Among those most responsible for the success of the annual First Flight ceremonies at Kill Devil Hills were, from left, C. S. Meekins of Manteo, long-time Dare County Clerk of Court; the late D. Victor Meekins, editor-publisher of *The Coastland Times,* and the late Ralph Whitener, North Carolina native and executive secretary of the Air Force Association.

Wade Marr of Elizabeth City served for many years as master of ceremonies at the First Flight dinners, which usually featured speeches by noted aviation figures. Marr is shown here at one of the First Flight observances holding a portrait of the late Miles Clark, patron of the Elizabeth City High School Band, which participated in the ceremonies year after year.

A fixture of the First Flight observances is the laying of wreaths at the base of the granite marker on the spot where the first flight was actually made. Children, grandchildren, and great-grandchildren of witnesses of the 1903 flight participate in the wreath laying ceremony, as do members of the high school band from Elizabeth City.

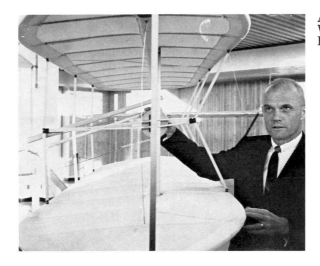

Astronaut John Glenn, shown inspecting an early Wright Brothers glider when he participated in the First Flight ceremonies in 1963.

Aycock takes a picture of photographer Bruce Roberts taking his picture of a couple of boys flying their kite at the Wright Memorial.

With a reproduction of the original Wright Flyer in the foreground Aycock got this picture of the Memorial through the windows of the Visitors Center.

The night of July 20, 1969, when the American astronauts were preparing for man's first landing on the moon, the National Park Service kept the Wright Memorial Visitor Center open, and a crowd assembled to watch the event on television.

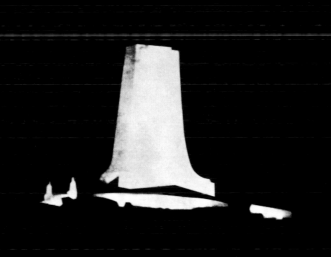

With portable radio in hand Aycock left the crowd at the
Visitor Center and walked to a spot where he could see
the moon above the lighted monument and at the exact
moment when man first set foot on the moon he took
this widely used photograph.

WORDS STEAM OUT
OF HIS MOUTH WITH A HISS
AND A SIZZLE

by Bill Wright
editor and publisher, *The State Magazine,*
Raleigh, North Carolina

The tourist industry in North Carolina had been underway for many years, but it had never soared. Irvin S. Cobb had come here in the mid-twenties, and had readily prescribed the missing ingredient: "All she needs is a press agent."

The fact was North Carolina already had press agents operating at full steam, but it was not until 1937 that the state of North Carolina officially undertook to proclaim its attractions to the world. That was the year the legislature authorized the North Carolina Advertising Division, and Governor Clyde R. Hoey gave the responsibility of setting it up to Bill Sharpe of Winston-Salem.

Whether by good luck or desire, the man chosen for the job was *not* an experienced press agent ("I had a quarter of a million dollars to spend, and didn't know the first thing about what they wanted"); but Bill Sharpe was a newspaperman from his head to his toes, and he believed in the persuasive power of a good story; and that, as it turned out, was even better. Within two years his news bureau was getting stories into out-of-state papers and magazines at the rate of five hundred a day.

It was a job that Bill obviously did not do by himself. On the coast there was Aycock Brown—a man who, unlike Sharpe, was not your classic journalist, but he *was* a born press agent. As described by Chester Davis, "...Aycock is not a sensational literary light. He is a man of unbelievable enthusiasm...that heats his thinking to a point where words steam out of his mouth with a hiss and a sizzle. In writing, Aycock has a tendency to fire words so fast that they climb up on one another's back and ride piggy-back.

"Give Aycock Brown sand and sea and water and he will make something newsworthy of it...whether it be a two headed turtle, a hurricane, a bathing beauty, or a bit of lore from the Outer Banks, it takes on freshness when Aycock tells a story and fires it out to editors...."

By the mid-thirties Brown was already a legend along the coast, and when Bill Sharpe came along, his amazing zest and energies gained a new dimension; the combination was unbeatable. Bill and Aycock remained close friends until Bill Sharpe's death in 1970.

A considerable factor in setting up North Carolina's surge to national attention was *The State Magazine.* Founded in 1933 by Carl Goerch—a New Yorker turned Tar Heel—the little (then weekly) magazine early identified itself with North Carolina's travel potentiality, and unquestionably helped to pave the way for the national publicity effort by declaring this state to its own people. It was predictable that Bill Sharpe would eventually become editor-publisher of *The State Magazine,* which he did in 1951.

The collected back issues of *The State* are, naturally, a good index to the life and times of Aycock Brown, beginning with a story about Simey O'Neal, a famed and flavorful character of Ocracoke Island, where Aycock had gone for a two-week vacation, stayed five years, and married a pretty girl named Esther Styron.

Next, Aycock is writing of a surprising catch of dolphin brought in from off the Outer Banks, far from the tropical waters usually associated with such fish. It was part of his crusade to let the world know that the Gulf Stream was not a Florida monopoly, but passes North Carolina only twenty miles from Cape Hatteras. We recall five years later that Bill Sharpe and his news bureau were still doing missionary work for North Carolina's Gulf Stream among the mass media, but it was Aycock who "discovered" it, and knew the sailfish and blue marlin were out there.

There were stories of wild goose decoys and knitting nets...of "goggle fishing" and the Gladiola Festival...of bathing beauties and the marine biology station...of hurricanes, shipwrecks, and a "Terrapin Derby"... lighthouses, wild ponies, yaupon tea, and Coast Guard heroes. Inland readers also learned about such salty characters as Stanly Wahab, of Ocracoke, and Tony Seamon the seafood czar, and Sam Jones who built the fabled Island Castle.

And in the meantime, Aycock edited the *Beaufort News,* established the *Ocracoke Beacon,* was press agent for the now Atlantic Beach development, and wrote bylined columns regularly for up-state newspapers. During World War II he was a special agent for the United States Naval Intelligence with the grim job of overseeing submarine warfare and its survivors along the North Carolina coast.

In the early 1950s the Dare County Tourist Bureau lured Aycock away from Carteret County and there was a noticeable shift in coastal date lines in the press, "because no coastal press agent has ever matched him in volume and durability."

Bill Sharpe, writing in 1967, recalls that, "One of the first pieces of national publicity on the Outer Banks appeared some twenty years ago in *The Saturday Evening Post.* One of the *Post* editors, Wesley Stout, stumbled onto the Outer Banks, and decided the region would make a good picture story. He asked Aycock if he would guide the *Post* photographer around on his tour. Aycock did so, but meantime he put together a story which he submitted to Stout. So instead of a photo layout with captions it became a text story with a few illustrations."

Again, writing in *The State,* Sharpe reminded his readers that "Dare is North Carolina's best publicized county. Of course, Americans have known for a long time about Kitty Hawk and Cape Hatteras. But it has been only in the last few years that these landmarks, together with *The Lost Colony,* the national seashore, Oregon Inlet, and Nags Head have been skillfully tied together into a region and attention focused upon it. The result has been the most extensive tourist development any single county has had in the past decade...."

"People in Dare are like folks everywhere, and some of them are inclined to believe that all of this development was the working out of manifest destiny. But those in the publication field and a few elsewhere know better. . . .

"If each county had an indefatigable and imaginative Brown to do its publicity, North Carolina very shortly would put the other forty-seven states right out of the tourist business."

Aycock has never had difficulty getting editors to print his pictures of pretty girls, probably because he usually comes up with unusual props, poses, or backdrops. In the late 1940s he made this widely used picture at the Croatan Hotel in Kill Devil Hills.

In the 1950s Carol Fulcher was one of Aycock's favorite Hatteras Island models. In this publicity picture the comely Buxton girl was gathering sea oats, since declared a protected species and thus protected by law.

Nationwide coverage was given to Aycock's pictures of the first "Shoe Checks" at Ras Wescott's Nags Head Casino. These girls were checking their "etc." as well.

Getting a good gimmick is half the battle in cheesecake photography. In this 1951 picture two pretty girls play catch on the beach with a large beach ball covered with stickers advertising *The Lost Colony*.

This dancer in *The Lost Colony* drama clasps Roanoke Island gardenias between her toes as she perches on the lowered mast of the play's "ship."

Sometimes the backdrop was pilings at a soundside dock.

Pretty girls and trees, especially gnarled old oaks, usually resulted in widespread publicity for the Outer Banks.

Other sure-fire cheescake backdrops were rail fences...

Lily ponds...

Outer Banks flowers...

and sailboats.

A favorite caption idea of Aycock's through the years has been to suggest that the *Lost Colony* Indian dancers looked more like Indians than full-blooded Indians born on a reservation.

With the growth of Nags Head as a resort area, fashion shows have become popular. Aycock is usually present, and usually gets his pictures published, as with this one of Anna Sadler from a recent Galleon Esplanade fashion show.

OUTER BANKS AYCOCK

by Hal Lyman
editor and publisher, *Salt Water*
Sportsman

When Sir Walter Raleigh's expedition reached North Carolina, it was doomed to failure as a colonization effort for two major reasons. First, Elizabethan regal politics had become so complicated that a follow-up trip did not materialize until it was too late. Second—and perhaps more important—Aycock Brown was not standing on the beach of his beloved Outer Banks to greet the group with camera and typewriter.

If Aycock had been at work, the course of history would have been changed and the Lost Colony undoubtedly never would have been lost at all. When a man can parlay a dead bluefish and an unshaven surf fisherman into a news story that reaches as far as Honolulu, just think what he might have done with cuddly little Virginia Dare toddling along the sands of Kitty Hawk!

When I first met Aycock more years ago than I like to consider, his glasses glinted in the North Carolina sunshine just as they do today. Around his neck, of course, was slung the inevitable camera. Perhaps there were two cameras, but my memory for such detail is poor. Before I really understood what was going on, I found myself posing for photo after photo, which cut into my surf fishing time considerably. Oddly enough, Aycock made it seem not only pleasure and entertainment, but also a part of my duty. Duty to whom or to what still escapes me, although he has succeeded with the same approach many times since. This talent of Aycock's has captivated people ranging from governors to beach bums, from shy octogenarian Outer Bankers to glamorous television stars.

From the point of view of an outdoor writer and magazine publisher, facts—with photos to illustrate these facts—are all-important when an article is in the planning stage. Time is always too short when making a trip to gather such material. Fortunately Aycock, nine times out of ten, can supply missing background information from his voluminous files. If he cannot furnish it immediately, he will dig it out from somewhere within a few days.

Many laymen do not realize that publicizing any area depends upon a variety of factors. Goodwill established with those involved in the media, whether they be magazine writers or television commentators, is the major one of these. If you do someone a favor, he in turn will reciprocate. An action photo needed in a hurry and supplied at short notice means that a "filler" photo or news release from the supplier at a later date will receive favored treatment. This is a sort of Golden Rule in the publicity game—and Aycock has built up a tremendous reservoir of goodwill.

Some involved with publicizing sections of our coast make it a practice to report only pleasant events. When tragedy strikes, when hurricane winds blow, or when fishing is terrible, these fair weather types become strangely silent. The result: those connected with the media become suspicious of any and all information received at any time. Aycock may not be happy about bad news, but he does not hesitate to report it.

It should be noted that his recovery powers are amazingly quick. Following an account of a new and unwanted inlet blasted through the Outer Banks some years ago, Aycock followed it almost immediately with an analysis of the possible benefits it might have on fishing if the inlet remained open! Nature fortunately never challenged that analysis because the inlet filled.

Aycock Brown would never have been a success on Madison Avenue. He has to know his subject thoroughly, which is impossible in that area. He knows and loves the Outer Banks and has helped countless writers to reflect that knowledge and affection.

When the time finally comes and Charon is ferrying him across the River Styx, I can see those twinkling glasses and friendly grin brought into play once more.

"Just lift that pole a little higher, Charon," he will say. "The scenery is interesting, but I sure wish the Wright Memorial were in the background. Have you ever been to the Outer Banks?"

Throughout Aycock Brown's more than a quarter of a century of publicizing the North Carolina Outer Banks he has demonstrated amazing photographic versatility. In thousands of pictures taken each year he has recorded good news and bad, major events and minor occurrences. Some of his pictures are distributed by the photo services and printed in hundreds of newspapers. Others are designed only to be used by the home town weekly, to provide proud proof of a fisherman's catch on an Outer Banks vacation. Here is a representative sampling of his work.

When former *Lost Colony* actor Andy Griffith spoke at an annual meeting of the Dare County Tourist Bureau, Irene Smart Rains surprised Andy by presenting him with the sword he had worn as Sir Walter Raleigh during the early 1950s.

To publicize the opening of the Duck Woods Golf Course, first on the Outer Banks, Aycock used a pretty girl, Sanfra Ange, and a beach businessman, Wayland Sermons, as models, neither knowing nor caring whether their attire was proper for the activity.

A widely used picture publicizing the Dare Coast
Pirates Jamboree.

A rough sea pounds against the remains of one of two
LST's which foundered on the Outer Banks in the early
1950s.

Elvira Payne inherited the job of drum beater in the Old Christmas Celebration held annually on the fifth of January at Rodanthe.

A typical promotional picture of *Lost Colony* Indians celebrating the "corn harvest."

A United States Coast Guard lifeboat demonstration on Hatteras Island in the mid-1950s.

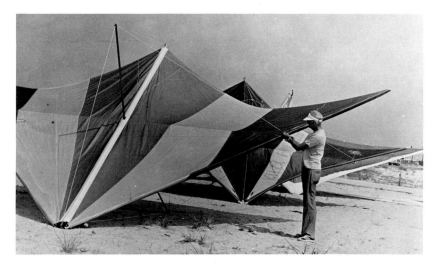

Francis Rogallo, inventor of the Rogallo Wing and pioneer in hang gliding, has retired at Southern Shores near Kitty Hawk, and helped make Jockey's Ridge one of the first places in the nation where hang gliding became a major attraction.

This unidentified shipwreck was uncovered on the shifting sands of south Nags Head Beach. Scientific studies determined that she was probably of pre-Civil War vintage, and then the same surf which had exposed the wreck, within a month had covered her again.

The Ocracoke bound *Herbert C. Bonner,* one of the early toll-free ferries operating on the Hatteras Inlet run.

A news picture of storm damage following one of the hurricanes which struck the Outer Banks.

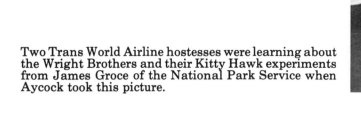

Two Trans World Airline hostesses were learning about the Wright Brothers and their Kitty Hawk experiments from James Groce of the National Park Service when Aycock took this picture.

Mounted Ocracoke Boy Scouts attended a Hatteras Island Pirate Jamboree celebration on their banker ponies.

Duck hunting has long been popular on the Dare coast.

Aycock's son Brantley, then a merchant seaman, bought this beret for his Dad in Italy; but Aycock got so much ribbing when he wore it during a first flight celebration that he retired it for good. (Photo by Jack Williams)

A *Lost Colony* publicity picture, featuring pretty girls and an Outer Banks beach.

A closeup view of the Cape Hatteras Lighthouse, with the abandoned Keeper's quarters, now a National Park Service Museum of the Sea, in the background.

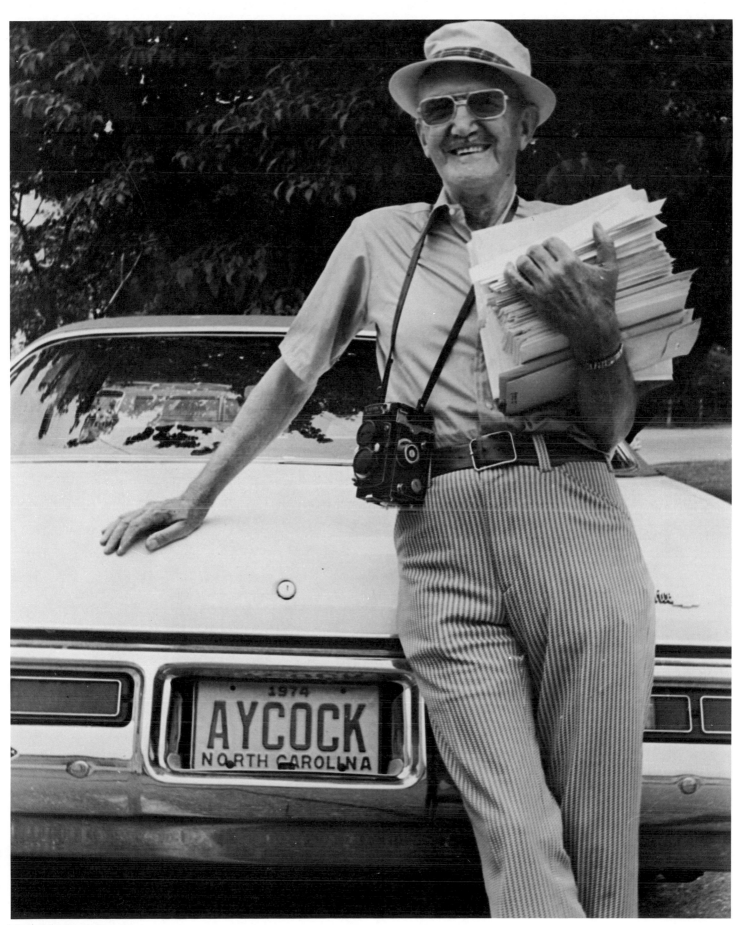

(Photo by Ray Couch)

David Stick's enthusiasm for the history of North Carolina is evident in *Aycock Brown's Outer Banks* as in his previous books *Graveyard of the Atlantic, The Outer Banks of North Carolina,* and, with Bruce Roberts, *Cape Hatteras Seashore.*

The preparation of *Aycock Brown's Outer Banks* was of special importance to David Stick, who joins with other members of the Dare County Tourist Bureau and the residents of and visitors to the Outer Banks in appreciation for Aycock Brown's over 25 years of publicizing the excitement and beauty of the Outer Banks.

David Stick is a member of the Dare County Tourist Bureau and chairman of the North Carolina Coastal Resources Commission. An active supporter of library development, he was the first president of North Carolinians for Better Libraries in the 1960s and chaired the Legislative Commission to Study Library Support in North Carolina.

ADDENDUM

Aycock Brown died April 13, 1984, half a year short of his 80th birthday; but his legacy remains. The Aycock Brown Welcome Center at Kitty Hawk, a joint venture of the State of North Carolina and Dare County, serves thousands of Outer Banks visitors each month. Appropriately, it is operated by the Dare County Tourist Bureau, which Aycock managed so effectively for more than a quarter of a century.

Aycock would like the appearance of the building housing the visitors' center, for it sits atop a sea-oats adorned sand hill, and its design incorporates the features of the old lifeboat stations about which he wrote so often and eloquently. And he would like, even more, the emphasis of this facility which carries his name, for he had come to realize that the role of the Tourist Bureau had changed and that its efforts in the future should be concentrated on informing and assisting the multitudes of tourists who now come to the Outer Banks.

I think Aycock would have been pleased, also, that the three men who incorporated the Tourist Bureau 35 years ago—Lawrence L. Swain, Wallace H. McCown, and I—and his long time assistant Sarah A. Owens, have established an Aycock Brown Memorial Fund in the Outer Banks Community Foundation, and that all profits from this reprint of *Aycock Brown's Outer Banks* will be added to this fund, providing scholarship aid for those who might want to follow in the bigger-than-life footprints of Charles Brantley Aycock Brown.

—David Stick
Kitty Hawk, North Carolina, Summer 1986